ADRI

GW01454516

and the
Thirty Nine
Steps

by

Margaret Cave

Romanian Aid Fund 1993

Adriana and the Thirty Nine Steps

British Library Cataloguing-in-Publication Data.
A catalogue record for this book is available from the British Library.

ISBN 0 9522586 0 9

Grateful acknowledgement is made to BLESMA for the permission to reproduce material on page 70 from *Better Health for the Amputee* by H E S Pearson MD FRCP.

Printed and bound in Great Britain by
Flair Press, Northampton
for the
Romanian Aid Fund,
1 Catherine Court, Buckingham, MK18 1UG.
Typeset by *Romanian Aid Fund* using *Calamus* running on an Atari Mega ST computer.

Dedication

To Adriana

for her courage in allowing her story to be told.

"For I know the plans I have for you," declares the Lord, "plans to prosper you and not to harm you, plans to give you hope and a future" (Jeremiah 29 v 11).

Acknowledgments

There was no way of knowing that the letter from Romania which dropped through our letter-box in May 1990 would turn the next few years into such a frenzy of activity; or that, in the process, I would make so many new friends.

Those of us involved in the day-to-day work with Adriana were left with a sense of wonder as we were privileged to see God at work at such close quarters. Such interest in her progress had been shown by so many people that I felt it necessary to try to compile a report once she had returned to Romania. Even some members of our own church were not fully aware of all that had been happening. This book is the result.

The whole project depended on teamwork and I would like to thank all who have been involved in the story of Adriana's rehabilitation.

The book could never have been written without Roy's love, support and encouragement. Andrew lent his journalistic expertise and steered me through the initial stages. Wendy and Mark, Dad and Margaret encouraged me to keep going.

I would like to thank Grace, Anne and Sheila, who made up the 'Adriana Committee' and shared the bulk of the work involved; their husbands, Stuart, Ken and Peter who, as well as sharing their homes, shared some of the pain and frustration at times; Fred, for his help, guidance and patience in reading, re-reading and helping to shape the manuscript; and the two Davids and Laurence for their help in the final stages. Thanks too to all at Whaddon Way for their prayers, interest and support all the way through.

We are especially grateful to Bob and Tessa Watts and the staff at Dorset Orthopaedic; to Geoff Miller and the physiotherapists Ann Dring and Mary O'Byrne who gave their professional expertise in the practical side of Adriana's rehabilitation and Saxon Clinic for the use of their gym facilities.

Valerie Hornsby was a valuable sounding board when things were difficult and always seemed able to find a possible solution. Pat and Ronnie Boyd and Colin and Mary Boocock were a constant source of practical help and encouragement.

The *Baptist Times* helped us get our appeal off the ground by their coverage of Adriana's story as it unfolded, as did Barry Amis of BBC Radio Bedford. The Limbless Association, BASA and BLESMA all provided valuable advice when it was needed. George Buckley and the Rotary Clubs of Ferndown, Parkstone and Bletchley gave help freely and generously.

The staff and pupils of White Spire School and Thornton College welcomed Adriana, loved and encouraged her and continue to take an interest in her progress.

A final thanks to all those churches, organisations and individuals who responded to our appeal to give Adriana a new start. They are too numerous to list but we are grateful for their prayerful and practical support.

Margaret Cave, Bletchley, October 1993.

Contents

1: The accident

It was still dark and cold when Adriana Dobre was woken from a deep sleep by her older sister, Simona, shaking her shoulder. She pushed her long dark hair away from her face as she sleepily enquired the time. "Half past four," whispered Simona, "time to get up". Adriana groaned, then yawned and stretched before swinging her feet out of bed. As they touched the floor she shivered, partly from the cold but mostly from excitement as she contemplated the day ahead.

It was April 30th 1990, a public holiday. 4.30am seemed an early start to the day but she was not too worried about that. She had recently reached the magic age of sixteen and, for the first time, was being allowed to join the group of young people from her church on a day walking in the Carpathian mountains, a two-hour train journey from her home town of Ploieşti (pronounced 'Ployesht') in Romania. Although she had been with the young people's group before, it had always been under the watchful eye of one of her older sisters. This time she was going in her own right as a full member of the youth group.

Their younger brother, Iosif, still had more than a year to go before reaching his 16th birthday. He had been trying for days to persuade them to take him with them, but Adriana and Simona did not want the responsibility of a younger brother tagging along to spoil their fun, so they had refused. Now they crept about quietly, trying to make certain they didn't wake up the other members of the family, especially Iosif who would probably renew his pleas. Their mother, Olga, was already in the kitchen making up the packed lunches of bread, tomatoes and cheese they would require for the day. Once they'd stowed it all into a knapsack, they let themselves out of the front door. There were no lights on the staircase so they needed torches as they crept quietly down the 39 steps which led from the door of their second-floor apartment to the pavement.

The train would be leaving at 5.30am from Ploieşti-West station about one kilometre from their home in Strada Malu Roşu. As there were no trolley-buses running at that early hour the girls set off on the twenty-minute walk to the station. As they walked, the rain fell steadily. Not a particularly good start to the day, they thought, as they walked along trying hard to avoid the potholes in the pavement which were rapidly filling with water.

Simona needed to walk more slowly than Adriana because the pair of shoes she was wearing did not fit very well and she was also carrying the heavy knapsack needed for the day. As they neared the station, they heard footsteps behind them and a voice called "Wait for me!" As the tall thin figure of Iosif appeared out of the darkness and came alongside they realised all their efforts had been in vain. There was nothing else they could do now but take him with them.

Tired of walking at a snail's pace on the wet streets, Adriana and Iosif ran on ahead to buy the tickets. Iosif took his and went off to find the other boys, while Adriana met up with her friend, Raluca. Chatting excitedly, they made their way on to the platform to find the rest of their friends. Adriana had arranged to meet up with Simona on the platform but, as the train was already in the station, Raluca clambered up the three steep steps into the carriage from the ground-level platform and stood by the door. They carried on chatting while Adriana kept a look-out for Simona.

Iosif and his friends had already jumped on board and were soon lost among the other youngsters who were scattered throughout the train, looking for seats. It was still dark and Adriana peered into the blackness trying to see whether or not her sister had arrived and boarded a carriage further back.

Suddenly the train began to move. The carriage door was still open. "Hurry up!" cried Raluca "or it will go without you. Here, grab hold of my hand and I'll pull you up." Adriana held up her hand as she began to run alongside the train. Her friend leaned out of the train to grasp it, but Raluca did not have the strength to pull her up the three steps and had to let go. Adriana stumbled and was quite unable to stop herself from falling. To her horror she found herself slipping underneath the train.

There was a sharp pain - and then nothing but warmth. She was not to know at that stage that the warmth was that of her own blood. She concentrated hard on not allowing herself to be pulled completely underneath the train as she felt herself being rolled over and over by the suction created by the movement of the carriages. In her panic she prayed: "I am going to die. Please, Lord Jesus, save me!"

Adriana, the sixth of nine children in a church-going family, had not made her own Christian commitment, but she naturally turned to prayer as the only source of help in this desperate situation. As she fought to remain conscious, she counted seven coaches of the train as they passed over her legs.

The train went on its way to the mountains, with none of its passengers aware of the tragedy that had just taken place - except Raluca. Incredible as it may seem, she carried on as if nothing had happened. There are occasions when the brain refuses to accept the message it is receiving and the horror is just too much to take. To Raluca, Adriana must have been killed and there was nothing she could do. Shock obliterated the tragedy. She said nothing.

Iosif, already on the train, was also quite unaware of the tragic accident taking place. He recollects the train having a rather bumpy start to the journey, but did not know the reason until they all returned from their day out.

Two men, who had seen what had happened, ran to Adriana's side and lifted her from the track on to the platform, where Simona, arriving late, footsore and breathless, found her. An ambulance was urgently summoned. Adriana was losing a lot of blood but was still conscious. As the minutes ticked by, Simona pleaded in desperation with the people arriving for the next train for someone to take them to the hospital in one of their cars. Her pleas fell on deaf ears. Cars are not easy to come by in Romania. No one was willing to get their car messed up by taking the injured girl to hospital.

The ten minutes until the police arrived seemed like an eternity but there was still no sign of an ambulance. The policemen called again for the ambulance but it did not arrive until more than twenty minutes after the accident had happened. Adriana was lifted in and Simona climbed in after her. Still there was no real pain - just the warm feeling. "Have I lost my feet?" Adriana asked Simona, who could only nod dumbly and hug her tighter.

By the time they arrived at the hospital, Adriana had lost three litres of blood. She was given a massive blood transfusion and her mangled legs were operated on immediately. She knew she had lost both feet but was not prepared for the shock of discovering, when she came round from the anaesthetic, that one leg had been amputated just below the knee and the other high up by the pelvis. The family, to this day, have never had it explained to them why such severe amputation was necessary.

2: The background

Bletchley, in the heart of leafy Buckinghamshire, is a world apart from the pollution-laden skies of the Romanian oil town of Ploieşti but a fragile link had been forged eight months before Adriana had her tragic accident.

Three months before the Romanian Revolution in December 1989, I flew to Bucharest with my husband, Roy, who is Baptist minister at Whaddon Way Church in Bletchley, a part of Milton Keynes.

It was our first visit to an Eastern Bloc country, to encourage the Christians oppressed by the regime of the tyrannical Nicolae Ceauşescu. As far as we knew it would be a once-in-a-lifetime experience, but the old saying that God works in mysterious ways was never to be more true.

I first became involved in the plight of persecuted Christians in Eastern Europe during Roy's fourteen-year ministry at Arbury Road Baptist Church, Cambridge, when I read the book, *The Siberian Seven*, by John Pollock. The story of how these committed Pentecostal believers were being used as pawns between the two Superpowers spurred me into a kind of political lobbying I had never anticipated. Helped by the national campaign to free the Seven from their basement prison in the American embassy in Moscow, I formed a group in our church and we started to make our own protests heard.

Described by our local newspaper columnist as 'hurling frail paper darts at the walls of the Kremlin', we kept on campaigning until the Seven and several other prisoners of conscience were released, establishing a warm camaraderie in our little group.

By the time that Roy was appointed as Chaplain to Willen Hospice in Milton Keynes, linked to the pastorate of the small Baptist/Anglican church nine miles away, my heart was well and truly in Eastern Europe. As we prepared to move in September 1988, I didn't know what I was going to do without our faithful little support group at church. I knew no one in the Bletchley area who was involved in Eastern Europe but had noticed that the Romanian Aid Fund held their annual conference in Milton Keynes so wrote to the treasurer and said I hoped that I might be able to get more involved with their work once we were in their area. A few days after we moved into our new Manse, I received a letter from Valerie Hornsby, Secretary of the Romanian Aid Fund whose office is in Buckingham, 12 miles from Bletchley:

"We have heard that you are moving into our area and wonder if you are the answer to our prayer. We are needing someone to come to work in our office to help with the administration for one day a week."

I didn't know if I would be the answer to their prayer but they were certainly the answer to mine.

Within a couple of weeks I had started in the office in Buckingham and after less than a year we were sent to Romania to 'get the feel of the country and meet some of the Christians'. Our brief was simple, as befits novices. We were to fly to Bucharest and travel around Romania by the cheapest and most efficient form of transport - train. We would visit a number of the churches and our ministry was to be one of encouragement, to assure the Christians that they were remembered in the prayers of many people in the West. One of the cities we were asked to visit was Ploieşti.

Many people travel through Ploieşti but few seem to visit. We tried to do some background reading and found a couple of travel guides in our local library. Ploieşti sounded a pretty grim place. Oil refineries surround three sides of the city and on the fourth there are chemical works - so whichever way the wind blows . . . One book dismissed Ploieşti in one sentence as not worth a detailed investigation unless you have an interest in the oil business.

We learned that Ploieşti was where one of the world's first oil refineries was established in the last century. In 1916 the oilfield was destroyed by British agents, to deny it to the Germans. Ploieşti was again carpet-bombed in 1944 by allied aircraft. It has been rebuilt as a 'concrete city' and seems to have the distinction of being one of the most polluted cities in Romania. It certainly did not sound like a holiday resort. The only tourist attractions listed were a clock museum and the infamous Doftana Prison a few kilometres outside Ploieşti, which was, apparently, a 'place of torture and confinement for participants in the 1907 peasant rising'.

At that time the Romanian Aid Fund (known to its supporters as RomAF) had no personal contacts with the churches there and we were to try to make contact with the Baptist Church. Shortly before we were due to go a letter arrived at the office from one of our RomAF supporters, Pat Boyd of Seaford in East Sussex. She had been writing to a Romanian family for some time and wished to send them a gift but wanted to make sure it arrived safely. At that time, parcels to Romania often did not arrive at all. Could we offer any suggestions? The family to whom she was writing were members of the Baptist Church - in Ploieşti. Of course we offered to take the parcel for her.

Our luggage was filled to the maximum allowed weight with soap, toothpaste, tights, headscarves and other such 'luxuries' donated by our church members. We, in turn, gave them our proposed itinerary. We have never been so conscious of being surrounded by prayer as we were during those two weeks in Romania.

We found a country where time seemed to have stood still for the past sixty years. Bucharest used to be called 'The Paris of the Balkans'. It was easy to see that it had once been a very beautiful city which had been destroyed partly by neglect and partly by the grandiose schemes of President Ceauşescu. He had ripped away its heart to build his enormous white Palace of the People and the boulevards of extravagant apartment blocks for his many relatives and party favourites. The air of oppression was almost tangible. No one smiled. No chattering groups met on street corners. Everyone walked with head down, shopping bag in hand, just in case food was to be found. No eyes met ours as we walked the streets, yet we were conscious that we were the focus of many eyes, however hard we tried to blend into the background. The only people who acknowledged our existence were the beggars, and those who wished to buy our currency illegally, either in the street or in the hotels.

The careful briefing we had been given stood us in good stead. We had various people to see and messages to pass on, all of which we had carefully coded and were kept on our person at all times. All our comings and goings in the hotel were noted by the cleaning lady on the corridor and the men in dark overcoats who lurked around the hotel reception area. Ordinary Romanian citizens were required to report any conversation with a Westerner to the police immediately.

The economic situation was just as desperate as we had been told. Potatoes, flour and sugar were strictly rationed. Milk was only available to children under three years of age (1 litre every two days - if you could find it). Butter, cheese and coffee were only available in the dollar shops to which the ordinary citizen had no access as it was illegal to hold foreign currency. Butchers shops were empty; market stalls might as well have been, as the produce displayed was so poor. Medicines, even basics such as aspirins and Vaseline were unobtainable. Petrol was severely rationed - when available. Streets and shops were unlit; roads unmade. Everywhere there was an air of neglect. There was also a shortage of building materials as they were all being used to throw up horrendous concrete apartment blocks, many of which had only communal washing and cooking facilities in the basement. All the best materials were being used to build the palace.

After three days in Bucharest we travelled on by train to Ploieşti and booked in at the Hotel Prahova. The next day, using an old street map of the town, on which many of the road names were different, plus a sketch map Pat Boyd's Romanian pen-friend had enclosed in a letter, we set off to find his apartment and deliver her gifts for the family.

After a long walk carrying a very heavy bag in the 90-degree heat, we found the apartment block and went in the front entrance. Once inside there was total darkness: no light bulbs on the stairs, no windows on the landings, just blackness. We felt our way upstairs to what we hoped was the right apartment and knocked on the door. It was opened by a slightly-built young man who we guessed would be in his early thirties. "Vasile Necula?" we asked in a whisper, conscious that at any moment one of the neighbouring doors could open. "Da" (Yes) he replied cautiously. A whispered explanation was needed. "We are from England, from Pat Boyd." His puzzled expression gave way to dawning comprehension and he quickly beckoned us inside and closed the door, but not without a quick check to make sure we had not been seen or overheard.

Once inside we were ushered into the living room where we introduced ourselves properly. A small, chubby-faced young woman with short dark hair approached us with a shy smile. "My wife, Fabiola" (Faby), Vasile introduced us proudly; then, equally proudly, "My children, Sergius and Emanuel" as two small boys sidled into the room and regarded us with saucer-like brown eyes.

We were completely ignorant of the special significance this meeting would have for us and our church in the not-too-distant future. Faby was one of Adriana's older sisters.

Vasile had only a few words of English and we had even fewer of Romanian. After we had greeted them and the other members of Faby's family who kept arriving - news spreads quickly - we handed over the gifts. Then Vasile got out his Bible. We read the Scriptures and prayed together - they in Romanian, we in English. Cups of coffee arrived for us and while we were drinking, Vasile was desperately sending out messengers to try to find someone who could interpret for us. No one was available and we had to manage with a smattering of French and Vasile's English.

Eventually we were informed that we were all leaving. "No speak on stairs!" said Vasile, with a finger to his lips as he first peeped through the spy-hole in the door to make sure the coast was clear. We crept down the stairs, trying to be as quiet and inconspicuous as possible as the shapes of other people passed us on the way up. Once outside, we were told again "No speak!" as we were led to the trolley-bus stop. By now the sky had turned dark and gloomy and rain was falling. We had no idea where we were going but followed Vasile and Faby dutifully on to the trolley-bus where they did what was necessary as far as the tickets were concerned and not a word was exchanged between any of us until the bus stopped and they alighted and we followed. Once we were in the street we could speak again.

At last we turned into the entrance of another of the concrete apartment blocks which seemed to line every street. Up two more flights of stairs, guided by the dim light of Vasile's torch until we stopped by a door at the end of one of the landings. Faby stepped inside, motioning us to follow, while Vasile brought up the rear. We had arrived at the home of Faby's parents, Peter and Olga Dobre. Olga appeared in the hallway and greeted us with a wide smile and outstretched hands. "Pace" (Peace) she murmured as she took my hand in a firm grip and kissed me on both cheeks. "Pace" (pronounced 'pachay') is the greeting used among Christians in Romania whenever they meet. I felt immediately at home with this warm, friendly woman, who proceeded to take charge of the situation. We were ushered into the living room where Peter stood. Stockily built, with the complexion of a man born and brought up in the countryside, Peter was a man of few words even in his own language. He smiled a welcome and once more our hands were encased in a warm grasp as he motioned to us to sit down.

Here, we discovered, there were even more comings and goings than in Vasile's apartment, although most of it appeared to be comings rather than goings. The word had spread quickly. We soon discovered that Olga had eight other children apart from Faby and it wasn't long before five of them had turned up, closely followed by Olga's mother, a widow who lived just a few blocks away on the same street. There were people everywhere but Olga took it all in her stride as her matronly figure bustled in and out issuing instructions to one and another.

The warmth of the greetings we had received was in stark contrast to the suspicion with which we had been regarded as we travelled by train or bus or walked into our hotel foyer. But then, as Christians, we were brothers and sisters with family ties that knew no barriers of race or language. Although Vasile still had not located an interpreter we soon felt as though we had known them for years.

Again we prayed together, Olga quickly grasping the nearest item to hand with which to cover her once black but now greying hair. It didn't matter whether it was a scarf, a tea towel or an apron but it is considered inappropriate for married women to pray with their heads uncovered. The Bible came out and we read the Scriptures together. Occasionally Olga would break into song and lead us through several verses of a hymn with her strong, tuneful voice. We discovered that many Romanian hymns are set to the old tunes we used to sing in our younger days, so we were able to join in with the English words.

In between issuing instructions, reading, praying and leading us in songs, Olga was rustling up a meal fit for a king. How did she do it? Food was practically unobtainable in the shops. She apologised that the meal was taking so long and showed me into her kitchen. There was a tiny two-burner gas stove. The pressure was so low that the flame was scarcely visible. On this slow burning flame she had to cook the family meals. But tonight the family were banished to we know not where and Roy and I ate with Vasile and Peter, the men of the family. We stood to give thanks, as is their custom, before settling down to enjoy the meal. Olga and Faby, we presume, ate in the kitchen, if at all.

After the meal was over, they hailed a taxi, as it was late and the trolley-buses were no longer running. "Ssh! No speak in taxi," said Vasile as it drew up outside the apartment. "I speak only." Once again we obeyed and sat in silence as he engaged the driver in idle chit-chat until we were a short, safe distance from our hotel. We all got out and Vasile pointed us in the right direction, then he and Faby melted into the darkness as we made our way to our hotel.

Neither Roy nor I slept well that night. The sense of oppression and the obvious caution taken by Vasile weighed on our minds. We did not want to cause them any problems with the authorities but we did want to make contact with their pastor and church if possible.

The next morning Vasile and Faby met us again at a prearranged spot. Faby had strict instructions to look after us and take us around the shops while Vasile continued the search for an interpreter. He returned triumphantly to tell us he had found one; Claudiu, the 14-year-old son of the pastor at the Baptist Church where both the families we had met were members.

This was marvellous news and meant we might have the opportunity to meet the pastor. Even better, when Claudiu eventually arrived, his father came too. We were the focus of a number of inquisitive glances as we stood, in the middle of an indoor shopping area, having an animated discussion about whether we could stay a day longer than planned as the pastor, Ioan, absolutely insisted that Roy should preach at the Friday prayer meeting. He was an imposing figure, with the air of one who was obviously used to getting his own way. We were only too glad to agree. Ioan politely but firmly took control of the rest of our time in Ploieşti. He took us home for a meal where we met his wife and his other two young sons and visited the church for choir practice. The English equivalent of his name is 'John' but it wasn't long before we had given him the nickname 'He who must be obeyed'.

As we looked around the packed church at the prayer meeting that

Friday evening we could already pick out familiar faces; Olga smiled and waved cheerily from her seat in the choir; Vasile, Faby and other members of the family nodded smilingly from their places in the congregation.

On our final morning in Ploieşti, Pastor Ioan insisted on picking us up at the hotel at 7am and taking us to the station for our train. We were very moved when we reached the platform, to find a group there to see us off, including Vasile and Faby with their four-year-old son Sergius, who was obviously wondering why he had to get up at such an unearthly hour to see two strangers onto a train. There were many hugs and kisses as we boarded the train and waved goodbye. It had been a very special time for us.We carried on with our planned journeying and met many more wonderful people in the other towns we visited, Braşov, Mediaş, Sibiu and on our return to Bucharest. They received us into their homes, introduced us to other Christians, prayed with us, shared their food with us, wasted their precious petrol on us - all the time going that extra mile. They are all very special people and we grew to love them all. Yet somehow it was Ploieşti that came back into our thoughts most often when we returned home.

3: We must send a lorry

We arrived home from our Romanian trip having fallen in love with the country and the people we had met who were shining like beacons amidst the darkness and oppression all around them. Yet we wondered how long the terrible situation there could continue before something tragic happened.

We couldn't wait to share the experience with our church. When they heard about the appalling conditions under which the people were existing, they wanted to do something practical to help. We started by sending food parcels to the people we had met. Some members gave money for food or to cover the very high postage costs; others brought packets of basic food items on Sundays. Every week I went home from church laden with carrier bags full of food. I was often glad that we only lived next door!

Our spare room soon began to resemble a small warehouse and Grace Miller, one of our church members, came regularly to help pack, seal, address and post the parcels. Obviously, some of them went to Ploieşti and we began to receive occasional letters from Vasile and Faby and Olga. We addressed each parcel as coming from a different church member, for security purposes. Soon those other members also began to receive letters from Romania.

In December 1989, just a few days before Christmas, reports began to filter through about an uprising taking place in Romania. It quickly became obvious that something very serious was happening, but what? We listened to every news broadcast to try to glean what was going on. We heard about fighting in Braşov, fierce fighting in Sibiu, shooting in Bucharest and as we listened we prayed for the safety of the Christians we had met in those cities. There was never a mention of Ploieşti. What was happening to our friends there? Had there been similar scenes of bloodshed in their town? There were no answers to our questions.

By Christmas Day I could stand the suspense no longer. I knew it would be no use telephoning Ploieşti as the possibility of getting hold of someone who spoke English was remote. Braşov had been in the thick of the fighting and we were anxious about the friends we had made there. It was not too far away from Ploieşti and they might have news. Trying to telephone anyone in Romania at any time was a very unreliable business. There was little likelihood of being connected - particularly in the middle of a revolution! - but I had to try. I picked up the 'phone, dialled the

Braşov number and, to my amazement, I heard the voice of the pastor, Gyula, say "Alo!"

"Yes, we are all safe," he said, in answer to my question. "There has been a lot of fighting here, but we had our service this morning and we have another this afternoon. We thank the Lord that we are having our first **free** Christmas!" As far as he knew there had been very little fighting in Ploieşti, although everything at that stage was still very confused and information was not easy to come by.

The rest of Christmas was wonderful!

After the revolution, there were months of total chaos as the people of Romania tried to sort themselves out and come to terms with what had happened. Now that the dreaded Securitate had better things to do than open people's mail, letters began to flow more frequently and we learned more about the writers and their families. Vasile must have kept the post office in business! He wrote to anyone and everyone. If he found an address on a piece of paper or the back of a book, he would write to it!

It soon became obvious that it was a waste of money sending parcels. The postage cost as much as, or more than, the goods inside. We heard of many towns being visited by lorries laden with aid but not once did we hear of anyone who had been to Ploieşti. Once again it seemed to be the town people only pass through en route to somewhere else.

Many churches started sending lorries to their own contacts in Romania. Why couldn't we do the same? Could we expect our small church, with less than 80 members, to take on such a big task? How would we start? Who would drive? How would we fill a lorry? I mentioned the idea to several people, particularly those who had taken a keen interest in Romania since our visit.

Peter Cutler, a schoolteacher, said he would love the opportunity to drive a lorry to Romania, but his wife, Sheila, would not go with him. He would have to go in the school holidays and it wouldn't be fair to her to take up his holidays in that way.

The weeks passed until one Sunday morning, talking to Ken Pitkethly, another member, I jokingly said, "Well, when are you taking our lorry to Romania?" "Any time," he replied, "but I don't know if Anne would be very keen on my going." "She could go with you," I replied. "Oh, no! You wouldn't catch Anne going to Romania." At that point, Anne, hearing her name, asked, "What wouldn't Anne do?" "Go to Romania, on a lorry," said her husband. "Who said so?" challenged Anne. "**You** did!" "I'll go, if you're going," said Anne. "Who else is going?" "Peter would go, but there's no way you'd get Sheila to go with him," replied Ken. Sheila happened to be passing at that moment. "I wouldn't go where?" "To

Romania - on a lorry!"

This was getting out of hand, so I intervened. "I have just asked Ken if he'll drive a lorry to Romania and he said he would. Peter has said he would like to go but that you wouldn't entertain the idea." "He's not going without me!" said Sheila. "Are you going, Anne?"

I knew, when I went home from church that morning that we would soon be sending a lorry to Romania! Within days I heard that Peter and Shelia's son, Nigel, would go with them in case they required a mechanic. Our team was fixed and the lorry project was under way.

From then on there was frenzied activity as we worked out the details. Our spare room became a hive of activity as boxes were packed and transferred into the church premises to make room for more. On the night before departure, the church youth group formed a chain to load the boxes on to the 7.5 tonne lorry we had hired from a local firm.

On Saturday, April 7th 1990, a large crowd gathered at church to commit our team into God's safe keeping and wave them on their way. Peter, Ken and Nigel were in the lorry, Sheila and Anne following by car. Neither of our intrepid ladies had ever driven on the continent before and here they were setting out on a three-day journey right across Europe.

Although the lorry stopped off at various places en route to drop off supplies to different people we had met on our travels around the country, there was never any doubt about its final destination. It was going to Ploieşti.

The team arrived in Ploieşti on Good Friday 1990 and spent Easter weekend with the pastor and members of Ploieşti Baptist Church. Before the terrible events of December 1989 it was illegal for any Romanian citizen to accommodate anyone in their home overnight, unless that person was a blood relative. In the new freedom they were just beginning to enjoy, they were now able to practice hospitality more openly and our team stayed in the homes of the pastor and members of the church.

After two weeks, the lorry and crew returned home safe and sound. We heard their stories and saw their pictures. Although they had neither met Vasile and Faby, who had gone away for the Easter holiday, nor had personal contact with the rest of the family, their visit forged another vital link between our church in Bletchley and the Baptist Church in Ploieşti.

We were soon to realise the significance of these links. Ten days after our lorry returned from Romania, Adriana had her accident.

4: The news breaks

The news that was to change the next two years of our lives arrived in the post on the morning of Thursday, May 10th 1990. On the mat was a letter from Ploieşti. When I opened it, I found it was from Olga, written by Vasile and translated into English by someone unknown. As I read it, my blood ran cold.

"Dear family,

Thank you very much for the gifts you sent us, but I had a great accident in family. My daughter, 16 years old, in the Railwai-station Ploieşti-Oest get off from the train and her feet are cut off. I talk with brother Cîmpean Ioan (their pastor) and he please you to leasten my sorrow.

Today brother Cîmpean had a family from England to him and together they visit my daughter to hospital. The family from England promised us that announce you about this. The church is very tested by this sorrow.

The family from England who was to Cîmpean promised me the fals feet from England for my daughter. I wish that you pray for me and my family much tested."

As I read the letter again to allow the full import to sink in, the telephone rang. Another church member, Doris Couper, had received a similar letter. So had a third member. We were all stunned. Questions ran around in our minds. Which of the daughters was the 16-year-old? What kind of treatment would she be able to get in a Romanian hospital? What about the risk of infection? How had the accident happened? Was there anything we could do to help?

Some weeks previously Doris had received a letter from Olga. In answer to one of Doris's queries, Olga had listed her children and their ages. We found the letter and read it through again:

"Gina, (28) married to Ionel: 4 children; Fabiola (Faby), (25) married to Vasile: 2 children; Nicoleta, (22) mentally retarded; Camelia (Lily), (20); Simona, (18); Adriana, (16); Iosif, (14); Magdalena (Magda), (12); Ovidiu (Bibi), (8)."

It must have been Adriana who had had the accident. None of us had met Adriana - she had been away on a school field trip when Roy and I visited the family in 1989. For some reason, Olga had enclosed a small photograph of one of her children with Doris's letter - a small, black-and-white, passport-sized picture. When we looked at the name on the back we realised it was a photograph of Adriana.

At the RomAF office I shared the news of the accident with Valerie. She was as horrified as we were. Sadly, it is a fairly common type of accident in Romania. "What can we do?" I asked. "Is there any chance of her having artificial legs fitted in Romania?"

"I very much doubt it," was the reply. At that time, Valerie and her family were making arrangements for Maria, another Romanian girl, to come to England to have a very basic artificial leg replaced. Maria lost her leg some years ago and had a very rough artificial one which required a heavy canvas shoulder harness. She could never wear a skirt or a pretty dress as the leg was not suitable to be 'on show'. Who better than Valerie to advise about the possible costs of artificial legs. A quick calculation, based on the costs for Maria, revealed that we would probably need at least £4,000 if we wanted to help Adriana obtain her 'false feet'.

A small church such as ours, worshipping in a prefabricated building, could not think of a project like that. Valerie's family had had to wait until Maria stopped growing before they could replace her leg. Maybe Adriana would need to wait until she had stopped growing before she could be fitted with artificial limbs. If that was the case, it would give us a little longer to work out if we could help in some way.

More in hope than anticipation, I asked Valerie if she knew of any travellers going near to Ploieşti at that time. Vasile's letter had told us there had been some visitors from England at the hospital and I was anxious for more news about the accident. She gave me the names of Colin and Mary Boocock, from a church in Derby. These visitors mentioned by Olga could have been connected with any of the Christian agencies working into Romania - but they were linked with RomAF. As they were due home I took a note of their telephone number and rang them as soon as they returned. They were able to fill in a few more details from what they had learned on their visit to the church and the hospital. They had promised the family that they would do what they could to help.

"Perhaps we could work together," I suggested. "We shall have to take it to next week's church meeting first. However, Adriana will need a wheelchair, at the very least, as soon as she leaves hospital. Where on earth will we get hold of one of those?"

There was a short pause, then Colin said, "Gyula has some in his loft in Braşov, ready for distribution. They were a consignment from Norway, I believe. Perhaps we could somehow get hold of one of those."

By now, having heard more of the dreadful consequences of the accident, I was beginning to worry about the possibility of infection. I tried to imagine the pain Adriana must be undergoing and my mind jumped to "What about painkillers? Will the hospital have access to any?" The thought was too awful to contemplate. Suddenly I remembered Geoff Miller (no relation to Grace), a local surgeon who had shown slides of Romania at the *Night of Prayer for Eastern Europe* some months previously. He knew the conditions in Romanian hospitals and would be able to advise us. It was no sooner thought than dialled. I gave him all the details I knew and he advised what medication would probably be most suitable at this stage.

Armed with this information I rang Valerie. "Have we any travellers going out at the moment who could help with any of these?"

"Yes," she replied. "There's someone going very soon. I'll give them instructions to divert some of the medicines they are carrying to Adriana and to ask Gyula if we can have a wheelchair if someone goes from Ploieşti to collect it."

We had done what we could.

On Sunday 13th May, the news of the accident was announced in church - although the prayer-chain had been very efficient and most people had already heard. I visited the Bible Class to ask the young people to send Adriana some cards to cheer her up - but to be careful of the words. A 'hope you bounce back quickly' type of message would hardly be suitable. They were all pretty shaken at the news - after all, some of them were the same age as Adriana - and asked if there was anything they could send her. After a little thought they decided on a personal stereo and some tapes. She would be spending a lot of time sitting around and it would be good to have some music to listen to. They would empty their 'elephant' money box, which was used for charitable purposes, and see if they had enough money available. They had enough and to spare, so they bought her a pretty nightdress too to cheer her up!

Our church responded in their usual caring and practical way. After the service another teacher approached me. "The Junior Church would like to send something useful to Adriana but they can't afford a lot." Grace Miller, a nurse, had already discussed with a physiotherapist friend, the type of small aids that would be useful. She suggested a 'rope ladder' which attaches to the bottom of the bed and can be used by the patient to pull themselves upright, thus saving the family the hard work of lifting. Also, a 'handreacher', a stick with a grab on the end, to enable the patient to pick up items that have slipped on to the floor. The Junior Church felt they could cope with these small items and they were duly purchased.

Other members told me they had already sent cards and gifts by post. Our links with Ploieşti, and with this family in particular, were proving to be stronger all the time.

Two days later, on Tuesday May 15th, we were due to have our bimonthly church meeting. That morning I received a letter from Vasile:-

"Dear family . . . We don't know yet what's happened, how she had the accident. Adriana arrived under the wheels of the train and 7-8 wagens passed on her. She has not now, both feet. One foot is cut of from pelvis and one a little down from knee. In all that time she had and has her mind well.

I talk with brother Cîmpean (the pastor) and he implore you to help us in this problem . . . we are in impossibility to solve this problem in our country.

Please, excuse this appeal."

It seemed from this description of her injuries that the effect of the accident was even worse than we had imagined. Adriana had not just lost her feet, but also most of her legs. What an encouragement it was to read that 'she had and has her mind well' after such a traumatic experience.

At the church meeting we prayed for the family and discussed what we could do. I shared Valerie's estimate of £4,000 minimum for the cost of new legs. No one said, 'It can't be done', although the amount of money required obviously concerned the members. If other churches, such as Colin's in Derby, were to help and if we had to wait for Adriana to finish growing, perhaps we could help in some way after all.

We eventually voted to 'do all we can to help to raise the amount needed to give Adriana artificial legs', not exactly an earth-shattering, faith-filled decision. A little cautious, perhaps, but we were to discover very soon that it was just that little seed of faith and commitment that God was waiting for.

If we had known then the amount of work which would be involved and all the problems we would face, we would never, I am sure, have taken the matter any further. In that case, we should have missed out on the amazing experience of seeing God actively at work in the events which followed. We were just at the beginning - all that, was yet to come.

5: Preparations begin

In my role as Church Administrator and because of our personal involvement with Romania and the Dobre family, it was obvious that I was the one expected to start the ball rolling, so I wrote a letter about the accident and the amount we were hoping to raise and sent it to all four of the local papers. Romania was still very much in the news and there might be a few donations forthcoming to get us started.

I followed this up by visiting all the local shops, pub, garage and surgeries to see if they would take collecting tins for their counters. To my amazement, all except one agreed. Several church members also took them for their own work places. Having found all these willing contacts, Willen Hospice readily lent us some boxes for as long as we needed them.

All four of the local newspapers, having received my letter, rang within a period of one hour! Each one, of course, wanted to be the only one running the story while I wanted as wide a coverage as possible. The first paper to call wanted a photograph. The only one we had was the very small black-and-white photograph which had been sent to Doris Couper only days before the accident happened. It was very precious and was handed over on condition that it came straight back to us. That photograph was used for all our publicity purposes and was a very important factor in our appeal.

When the papers came out on May 24th we found we had made two front pages, a page two and a page three! More than that, a reporter on the *Milton Keynes Mirror* had made it his personal mission to contact some local firms to see if they would help and had managed to obtain a promise of £200.

Another of our church members had links with BBC Radio Bedford's Sunday morning programme *Melting Pot* and had made sure they knew about our new project, so I was soon being interviewed by the presenter, Barry Amis.

A letter, similar to the one sent to the local papers, was also sent to our denominational newspaper, the *Baptist Times*, and to all the local churches. A week or so later Roy and I attended a joint meeting of the Bletchley churches in Queensway Methodist Church, in the centre of Bletchley. At the end of the service, as we were leaving, I stopped in amazement as I saw Adriana's picture on the notice board. It was one of the cuttings from one of the local papers and two ladies from the church had already started raising money through their weekly coffee mornings!

The following week, six of us met at the Manse to pray together and discuss how to set about raising the funds needed. We all felt it was important that any money-raising for this project should not be allowed to detract from the Church's ongoing mission and outreach work. By the end of our meeting we had a list of suggestions to work on, ranging from sponsored bicycle rides to coffee mornings, a stall in Bletchley market and an entertainments evening by our young people.

As the result of another suggestion, free tubes of Smarties were offered in the church notices one Sunday morning. There was only one condition attached: the empty tubes had to be returned, filled with a selection of 1p, 20p or £1 coins. £5 and £10 notes were also acceptable! After the service I was besieged (and not only by the children!) and left church with a waiting list for Smarties.

A few days later the *Baptist Times* arrived and there was a beautifully enlarged copy of the photograph of Adriana. She was front page news again! Unlike all the other newspapers, they had managed to keep strictly to the facts as stated in my letter!

It was only one month since our church meeting had agreed to 'try to help'. Already I found I was spending whole afternoons or evenings on the telephone. We needed advice on all fronts. I had worked for four years in Cambridge in the office of a school for physically handicapped children, but that only heightened my awareness of how much I did **not** know about the needs of the disabled.

One afternoon I decided to contact the British Limbless Ex-Servicemen's Association (BLESMA). Adriana could hardly be called an ex-serviceman, but at that time they were the only relevant organisation I could think of and I hoped they would be able to put me in touch with someone who could advise us. After locating the number of their head office, I rang them. They were most interested and understanding, promising to send me some literature which might be helpful. They also gave me several useful addresses and telephone numbers, one of which was that of the head office of NALD, the National Association for Limbless Disabled, now known as The Limbless Association. I contacted them and spoke to the General Secretary, Mr Sladen.

I cannot speak too highly of the help I received from all the organisations for the disabled. I had many questions and was extremely ignorant of the kind of work they do. The more I thought about what we had taken on, the more I wondered if it would work. Would Adriana ever be able to walk again, even with artificial legs? Wherever I turned I found help and understanding of our situation from these specialist organisations.

Mr Sladen also sent me some literature from The Limbless Association, including some back copies of their magazine, *Step Forward*. One of the front page articles caught my eye. It featured a young lady called Jemma, also a double amputee, who had so conquered her disability that she had taken part in a canoeing trip on the Boundary Waters in Canada. As her address and her telephone number were there, I contacted her. I really wanted to know if there was anything basic that would be of help to Adriana once she was discharged from hospital and back home in their apartment but we also talked about how Jemma coped with a job, drove a car and lived a very active life. She suggested that I send one of my appeal letters to The Limbless Association and ask if they would print it in the next issue of their magazine. She had received a great deal of help in that way when she was raising funds for her canoeing trip. It was no sooner suggested than done! I had no idea then just how far-reaching the result of that one 'phone call would be.

In response to the article in the *Baptist Times* donations were beginning to flow in. About a month after the launch of our appeal, we had received over £400. Donations, large and small, began to come from individuals, Women's meetings, Girls' Brigade companies, youth fellowships, churches, jumble sales, preaching fees, communion offerings and many other sources. Every day brought letters and cheques and just keeping abreast of the acknowledgments soon became almost a full-time job. By now, apart from my one day at RomAF I was also working three mornings a week at a local school. The days were becoming too short!

The two older church youth groups, 'Fish' and 'Chips', took part in sponsored cycle rides while the youngest section, 'Pickles', arranged a sponsored playground push, travelling from one play area to another.

One evening when I answered the telephone I heard a young man's voice. "Are you connected with the church that is raising money for a Romanian girl who has lost her legs?"

"I am".

"Oh, thank goodness I've found you at last. I heard part of your Radio Bedford interview a few weeks ago but I didn't catch the name of the church. I've spent the last three weeks trying to find you. I want to help." That was music to my ears! The young man was Paul Wedrychowski (of Polish origin), organiser of a keep-fit club in the village of Castlethorpe to the north of Milton Keynes. He was offering to arrange a sponsored training session for our funds. "We can't do it until September and I don't know how many people will turn up, but every little will help," he said.

A doctor in Birmingham who was organising a Christian pop concert wanted to use the proceeds for Romania and contacted Valerie at RomAF. She suggested three projects, one of which was our appeal. It was encouraging to see the interest people were taking in our project even if it meant a lot of work providing promotional literature for such events.

By now, we were into July. The local supermarket had asked me to go and empty their box as it was already full! I popped into the Post Office and asked them if I should take theirs too as it was getting very heavy. "No, not until you bring an empty one to replace it", was the reply. "Today is pension day and that is when all the old folk pop their small change in. You'll miss a lot if you take it now." The sub-postmaster and his wife were Hindus but still wanted to help the local church. Many people felt the same way and it was just amazing to see their kindness and goodwill in action.

Our church folk marvelled as they saw a new total for the fund going up on the 'Adriana' notice board each Sunday morning. By the evening service it usually needed changing again! Money was still coming in from everywhere: a jam-jar at an Over-Fifties Club, collecting boxes taken to work, coffee mornings, and local schools and churches. Every morning Roy and I raced to pick up the post as letters and cheques, large and small, arrived.

Everything was gathering momentum and all thoughts of housework, baking and other such mundane matters were taking second place. I had the feeling I was being taken over.

6: Meanwhile – back in Romania

While all this activity was going on we had not had much news from Romania. We did hear from Vasile that Adriana had been transferred to the 'Urgency Hospital' in Bucharest five days after the accident happened. The transfer took place by ambulance and she was accompanied by her mother, Olga, and Ionel, the husband of her eldest sister, Gina.

When they arrived at the Bucharest hospital the doctors discovered that Adriana had developed infections in both stumps and it was necessary to take her to the operating theatre again to open up the wounds and drain the infection. It was understandable, given the circumstances, that the family had too much on their minds to bother about writing letters to England for a while. The letters we did receive were very short on news but full of faith in God and a touching and challenging belief in our ability to help them. As Vasile explained in his letter, "We are in impossibility to solve this problem in our country".

Through RomAF we found two travellers, Marie and Lois, who were going to Bucharest and were willing to take the gifts from the young people at church which certainly could not be entrusted to the normal postage system. Grace had managed to locate a book of physiotherapy exercises for amputees which we felt was important to get to Adriana as soon as possible. All we could tell Marie was that Adriana was in a hospital in Bucharest but we did not know which one. We did not even know when she had been admitted, so it was a difficult task for them to find her. Earning our undying gratitude, Marie, Lois and their Romanian friend combed every hospital in Bucharest, eventually managing to find Adriana and Olga and hand over the gifts. It was only when they came home that we heard about the infections which had developed. We had no means of knowing if the antibiotics and painkillers we had sent had arrived. We found out later that they had arrived in Romania, but they never reached Adriana. However the Bucharest hospital was able to provide her with the medicines and injections she needed to combat the infections. We were very pleased when we heard that Vasile had managed to arrange to collect the wheelchair from Braşov. At least something was happening.

During all this time Olga never left Adriana's side. The family brought a portable bed to the hospital and Olga slept on that, in the ward, by the side of Adriana's bed. Her sister Lily, who travelled to Bucharest to work in a railway carriage door repair workshop, brought food to them each day from Ploieşti as Adriana could not eat the hospital food.

It was while they were in Bucharest that the earthquake happened. Adriana was asleep in bed and woke suddenly to find her bed was shaking. She thought it was her mother shaking the bed and turned to ask her why she was doing it. But Olga had also been wakened and realised immediately what was happening. It was a frightening few minutes for everyone as everything rocked around them. They realised that if anything happened to the hospital they could die as their ward was on the first of eight floors. Olga had been through this experience before in 1981 when Ploieşti was shaken by an earthquake causing a lot of structural damage. Had Adriana survived such a tragic accident only to die in an earthquake? The thoughts must have raced through Olga's mind but after a minute or so, seeming like an eternity, the shaking stopped. Fortunately, little damage was caused to the hospital.

By the end of June, the doctors had decided that the stumps had healed and that Adriana was well enough to go home. "Take her home," they said to Olga. That was all. No social worker to call, no check-up in three months, no physiotherapy, no artificial limbs, no legs . . . nothing! Just "Take her home!" Home to what? To a second-floor apartment, up 39 stone steps, where a large family was already living. There was a balcony where she could get some 'fresh' air but it overlooked the dismal sight of similar blocks of grey concrete flats grouped around waste ground. Her panorama was one of rubbish skips, barren, uneven land and a post which is used for the Saturday morning ritual of beating the carpets!

There was nothing further the doctors could do for Adriana, and Olga had the distinct impression that there was no interest either. Her case was closed.

The family took Adriana home, decided a holiday would be a good thing for all of them and went off for a week to Predeal in the mountains. Once they had arrived at their destination, Adriana refused to venture out again until it was time to go home. Once home, that was where she preferred to remain. In Romanian society it is still considered a shameful thing to be disabled. Wheelchairs are rarely available and therefore not seen in the streets and there are no ramps or other facilities of any kind for the disabled. The only disabled people we had seen on our visit to Romania were the beggars, objects of pity or derision, shuffling along the train corridors, or wheeling themselves along the ground on small boards on wheels. That, plus the effort of having to be manhandled down three flights of steps (there is no lift in their apartment block) was enough to put Adriana off the thought of going out anywhere. She had occasional visitors but her school friends never came near and the young people from church only visited infrequently.

Due to the injuries she had received to her back at the time of the accident, Adriana was more comfortable lying down and therefore spent most of her time on her bed, watching TV or reading. If visitors did arrive, she made the effort to get into the wheelchair and wheel herself into the living room to see them, but that was difficult to sustain for long periods because it was so painful to sit upright.

Another problem was the fact that the wheelchair was too wide to go through the narrow bathroom door in their apartment, which meant she had to be carried there, with the resulting loss of privacy and dignity.

Humanly speaking, the future looked pretty bleak but Adriana and her family put their trust in God and believed that He would make it possible for her to come to England and to walk again.

Adriana's family:
Faby, Gina, Olga (mother), Lily, Nicoleta, Peter (father), Simona,
Ovidiu (Bibi), Adriana, Magda, Iosif

Photo courtesy of Colin Boocock

7: Back to Romania

By July 1990, less than three months into our appeal, we had already received over half of our target of £4,000. There was no doubt in our minds now that we would reach it sooner rather than later. There seemed to be plenty of time because we understood that Adriana would probably have to finish growing before she could have permanent limbs fitted. Otherwise, it would be necessary to bring her over to England again to have them changed once her growth was complete which would, of course, increase the difficulties enormously. It was suggested that her doctor would be able to advise when she had finished growing, which would probably be within the next twelve months, and it was possible that she would need further surgery before limbs could be fitted. Obviously that would have to be done on a private basis, normally a costly business.

Geoff Miller, the surgeon, was a great help. He had already indicated that, if further surgery was needed when Adriana arrived in England, he would be happy to perform the operation in the local private clinic and a consultant anaesthetist friend would also be happy to help. Both of them would give their services free of charge and he would negotiate a special price with the clinic.

We were growing increasingly anxious as the weeks passed. We knew that Adriana was home from hospital and that she was waiting for us to send for her to come to England but we were not yet ready for that. Mr Sladen of The Limbless Association had given me details of some of the firms which made artificial limbs. I remembered that, when Geoff Miller had shown slides of his visit to Romania at our *Night of Prayer for Eastern Europe*, he had mentioned Otto Bock, a German firm of limb-makers. I was pretty sure that he had said they had workshops in Romania. That sounded the best one to try first, so I rang their London office and asked if they could give me an idea of the cost. I didn't have anything like the amount of information they needed about Adriana's situation, of course! However, within two days I received a quotation, together with a letter asking me to telephone their managing director, Olaf Boyle, who wanted to speak to me.

Half expecting some sort of sales pitch, I telephoned. He was extremely helpful, asking many questions, pointing out many of the problems and answering many of the queries I had. We talked about our estimate of £4,000 which he felt should be sufficient providing there were no complications.

We still knew nothing about Adriana's situation and questions were constantly being asked by church members and others: will she have been given any temporary limbs? Will further surgery be necessary? Will she be having any physiotherapy/walking training? How is she coping mentally? What will happen about her schooling?

We felt we were working in the dark and there were many times when, as the realisation began to dawn of what we were taking on, I felt "I'm out of my depth here. This is beyond me." The reply seemed to come "Trust me - I've got everything in hand."

It became obvious that we had to find out some of the answers to our questions regarding Adriana and the only way we could do that was for someone to go out to Romania, visit the family and report back. The cheapest way to go was to fly out on a two-centre package tour. This meant spending the first few days in an hotel at Mamaia on the Black Sea coast and then transferring to Poiana Brașov for the second week. Once in Brașov there would be no problem in leaving the group, travelling down to Ploieşti by train for a few days and then rejoining the group before they travelled back to Mamaia.

Roy and I couldn't afford to go abroad again and we certainly could not use any money from the fund but something had to be done because we were dealing with so many 'unknowns'. We were also learning once again that the Lord has His own ways of dealing with such matters, as various windfalls unexpectedly came our way. It was clear we were to go. Last year's trip to Romania had been, so we thought, a once-in-a-lifetime experience and here we were, only one year later, on our way again.

Olaf Boyle of Otto Bock instructed me to take as many photographs as I could of Adriana's stumps, from as many angles as possible. That sounded rather a tall order but I said I would try. Privately I wondered how a 16-year-old girl, whom I had never met, would react to such a suggestion.

The family was notified that we were coming, preparations were completed and on August 16th 1990 we boarded our flight for Constanţa on the Romanian airline, TAROM. The difference the revolution had made was apparent even as we boarded the aircraft. On the previous visit our passport had been carefully scrutinised by a grim-faced uniformed official who looked as though he wasn't too sure whether he ought to let us on the plane. This time we had our passport at the ready and it was not required; instead, smiling hostesses greeted us. Another difference soon became apparent. The curtain between the passenger cabin and the flight deck was open; we could see all that was going on in there. Not only that, but one of the passengers had a video camera and was given permission to go into the cabin to film the crew. This time last year, we mused, that would probably have led to summary execution! When we arrived at Constanţa the difference was even more marked. Everyone was smiling and helpful even though it was past midnight. As the coach took us to our hotel, forked lightning flashed over the sea and great peals of thunder rolled around - but there was no rain until we had all safely unloaded our luggage into the hotel.

As the past few months had been very busy, we made the most of our few days enforced rest by the Black Sea. We visited the Baptist Church in Constanţa and shared in the pastor's excitement at the installation of a small printing press in the basement. We also took the opportunity to visit ex-President Ceauşescu's seaside villa, which was open to the public. It was unbelievably opulent, especially when one realised that it was but one of around 80 such villas the dictator had built for himself, all of which were kept in a state of constant readiness, and few of which he ever visited. As we walked around, seeing the lake and the swimming pool and the fountains playing, it was hard to realise that this was in the same country where many people had no running water for most of the day.

Admiring the many exquisite Italian crystal chandeliers, all of which were lit, our thoughts went back to the thousands of apartment blocks similar to the one where Adriana lived where there was not a single bulb to light the way up the stone staircases. Even in the department stores, the goods on display were hardly visible and the tourist hotels often had no lights on the stairs above the third floor: light bulbs were unavailable in the shops and, before the revolution, each home was only allowed to have one 40-watt bulb in use at any time.

When we saw the beautiful indoor pool, where the water was constantly changed and filtered to keep it clear of infection and had been kept at a constant temperature of 80 degrees all year round, I was inwardly seething at the injustice of it all and could not resist defiling the germ-free water by surreptitiously dipping my foot, complete with sandal, into it!

Soon our four days of rest were over and we all piled on to the coach which was to take us first to Bucharest for one night and then on to Poiana Braşov in the Carpathian mountains, from where we could set out on our mission.

After a very tiring two-day journey we arrived at our destination. Poiana Braşov, which is situated about 12 km up the mountain from the beautiful old city of Braşov, is a purpose-built ski resort consisting of a large number of hotels, a few tiny shops and a bus station.

We telephoned our pastor friend, Gyula, in Braşov and soon we were in a taxi en route to see him again and to attend the Friday prayer meeting at his church. While we were there he offered to book our train tickets to Ploieşti for the following day and telephoned Vasile to say which train we would be catching. Now we began to feel that we were getting somewhere: the purpose of our visit was nearer fulfilment.

8: Ploieşti at last

At last, on Saturday 25th August, we boarded the train for Ploieşti. We had reserved seats as the train was pretty full. I am still trying to work out the logic in the numbering of the seats in that carriage. Standing in the doorway of the compartment, the four seats on our left were numbered '61, 63, 67, 65' and those on our right were numbered '62, 68, 64, 66'.

When we had travelled by train the previous year we were conscious of being watched. No one talked to us. Again the difference was apparent as we were offered chocolate, which we gratefully accepted, and the famous plum brandy which we refused as politely as we were able!

Two hours later, as we disembarked at our destination, we were greeted with hugs by Rebeca, the pastor's wife. Pastor Ioan with his son Claudiu who had previously interpreted for us, were making the most of the post-revolutionary freedom to travel and were in the USA. Vasile was also among the 'welcoming committee' and immediately took charge of our luggage as we were escorted to a car, driven by a member of the church. Two young people from the church had been searching for us on the train but it was so full they had had to give up until we all arrived in Ploieşti. Six of us piled into the car and were taken to the pastor's house where we were to stay. We dumped our luggage, had a quick 'cuppa' and got straight down to business. The first item on the programme was to go to visit Adriana's family.

We reached the apartment block. As before, there were no lights on the staircase. Once inside the main door, out of the bright sunlight, everything was in total darkness. Vasile carefully guided us up the stairs by torchlight and knocked on the door of the apartment. It was opened by Olga who threw her arms around me and sobbed on my shoulder. Words were superfluous. As before, we didn't need a common language. After all the trauma and worry of the past few months, they were tears of sheer relief that now something might happen to help Adriana. My tears mingled with hers for a few brief moments and then we walked inside together.

In the centre of their living room sat Adriana, in her wheelchair. She had obviously taken a great deal of trouble over her appearance and looked very pretty in a navy and white dress, with her long dark hair brushed back into a ponytail. She seemed rather shy and reserved. After all, we had not met before and who could know what was going through her mind about these English people? What were they like and what were they going to do to her?

The family had made arrangements for Catalin, an excellent interpreter from the local Pentecostal church, to be on hand. As we sat and talked, Olga gave us more details about Adriana's accident and we, in our turn, told them what was happening back in England. We explained that new legs would cost a great deal of money and gave Adriana a copy of the *Baptist Times* which featured our appeal and her photograph on the front page. We explained how we were hoping to raise the money and said that the doctors would need to check that she had finished growing before she could come. They understood the problem but informed us that the doctors had finished with Adriana. She would not be having any further check-ups and therefore they would have to guess when she had finished growing. We were stunned.

We prayed and sang together; then it was time to leave. "Will Adriana be coming to church tomorrow?" we asked. Olga looked shocked. "Oh no! She doesn't go out. She hasn't been to church since her accident." We ought to have guessed that but still found it hard to take in the Romanian attitude to disability. We just said, "What a pity! It would be good for her to go" and left it at that as we said our goodbyes and made our way back to the pastor's house.

On Sunday morning, Roy was to be one of the preachers. They already had a visiting preacher from a nearby town but an extra sermon from a visitor is something they always have time for. While Roy prepared for the service I, went to visit the Sunday School with a young man named Daniel as my interpreter. As it was holiday time, the numbers were somewhat depleted, but I had taken some Smarties as a small gift for the children. These were given out and the rest locked away in a cupboard. The children sang unaccompanied and in beautiful harmony. Suddenly the door burst open and two very breathless youngsters flew in, late. As they made their way to their places, the teacher spoke sternly to them. They turned and headed back towards the door. I watched, wondering if she was sending them home. No! They reached the door, opened it then closed it gently. Then they stood still, just inside the door and bowed their heads for a moment's prayer. Only then did they walk quietly to their places and sit down. I noticed them looking at the Smarties in the hands of the other children. Daniel said, "They will not be allowed to have any today."

Eventually it was time to leave the Sunday School and go into the church as the prayer meeting was finished and the morning service was due to start. As foreign visitors are treated as honoured guests, I was led up on to the platform to sit opposite the choir. Suddenly the door at the back of the platform opened and there to my astonishment was Adriana! The family must have gone to tremendous trouble to get her and her wheelchair down all those 39 steps from their front door to the street, into a car and then up the steps into the church. I was so moved to see her there and looked across the platform at Olga, who was in the choir. She was very near to tears again. What an ordeal it must have been for Adriana to sit there on the platform for the full two-hour service, in full view of the congregation, with no legs and nowhere to hide.

When the service was over, Adriana disappeared under a flurry of young and old who wanted to welcome her back. One of the first to greet her was her friend, Raluca, who had tried to lift her up into the railway carriage but had subsequently denied knowing anything about the accident. The truth had eventually come out and now it was with some trepidation that she approached Adriana. "Can you ever forgive me?" she asked. The reply came back immediately and unreservedly, "I already have".

How my heart ached for that young girl, who had lived with that burden for all those months. She had not dared to go and visit Adriana and her family. She needed care and counselling, as did Simona, Adriana's sister, who was obviously still deeply shocked by the whole episode.

The rest of Sunday was very busy. A coach load from the church was going to a village 70 km away from Ploieşti where, we were told, there were no Christians. Ploieşti Baptist Church had been asked to go to conduct an evangelistic meeting there by a young man who had been born and brought up in the village. He had moved away to Bucharest, where he had become a Christian. He was now a pastor and wanted to take the Gospel message to his home village so had asked his friends at the Ploieşti church to help. They had been there the previous month but the villagers were afraid of this new teaching and had driven them away with sticks and stones. They were not sure what would happen today, but were prepared for the same reception.

"Roy, you will preach?" said Rebeca! We both gulped! Was that a question or a command? While trying to come to grips with how I felt about that situation, I said, half in jest, "Well, we are told we must be prepared to suffer for the sake of the Gospel". Rebeca turned and replied very seriously, "It is our privilege". There was no need to say more. This is why the evangelical churches in Romania have remained strong under oppression and seen such growth.

We were due to 'phone home to report that we had met up with the family, so we took the opportunity to ask them for specific prayer for the village service. The church folk clambered on to a decrepit looking coach while we climbed into the jeep provided for the two preachers and various others and everyone set off for Florica, the village where the service would take place.

It was a very hot day and stifling for those of us crammed into the back of the jeep but it was an interesting journey. In many ways it was like travelling back in time as we passed through villages with wells in their front garden or by the side of the road. There were no hedges and the fields came straight out to the road. It was harvest time and where the grain was being harvested (by hand of course) there were little 'haystack houses' by the side of the road. These little dwellings were obviously inhabited. We were told that some of the workers slept there during harvest time to make sure no one stole any of the crop. There were also Gypsies, sitting by the side of the road, selling huge piles of water melons. The main road was not too bad but once we turned off towards the village it was nothing more than a dust track. The journey took us one and a half hours and by the time we arrived at Florica we were already hot, dusty and tired but the day was far from over!

9: Florica

The village of Florica consisted of a long, dusty, unpaved road with typical single-storey houses down each side. The street was deserted apart from one or two children playing and two old ladies who were standing chatting near the small Orthodox church. They eyed us curiously as we disembarked from the jeep and even more curiously as the bus drew up and everyone clambered out. The first of our party to arrive at the village hall, next door to the church, discovered that the door was not only closed but padlocked. There was obviously no way we were going to be allowed to hold the service in the hall that day. There was no suggestion that we retreat; we had come to hold a service. The choir formed outside the hall, the conductor raised his arms and they began to sing. As their beautiful harmonies soared out into the afternoon air, more people began to emerge from their homes to see what was happening. Soon practically the whole of the village had arrived. It was time for our service to begin.

Apart from a little vocal opposition at the beginning from one of the village elders - who was told by the villagers to go away and be quiet - the service proceeded without hindrance. The choir sang and the preachers preached. Roy preached first, followed by another Englishman. He was a builder, currently in Romania to help renovate an orphanage. He was followed by the pastor who had preached in the morning service in Ploieşti Baptist Church and the final preacher was the pastor who had been born in the village. The service lasted a good two hours in blistering heat, with only one tree providing any shade. Everyone listened intently. Even the children were attentive. At the end of the service the pastor asked if they could come again next month. The majority of the villagers raised their hands in invitation.

Before he prayed at the close of the service, this pastor announced that he had New Testaments and tracts available. Anyone wanting one could come to his car after the service. By the time the prayer was finished, his whole congregation was around his car. We had never witnessed anything like it. Hands reached out from the mêlée of people around the car and eagerly grabbed the literature offered. Of course, some of the children regarded it as a game to see how many pieces they could collect, but there were many who, having received a booklet, were walking quietly away, reading as they went. Others stayed to talk to members of the church. How we regretted not knowing the language well enough to enter into conversation.

On the way home, our jeep had a puncture. The pastor had a spare tyre but that too was flat. He had no pump and no jack. He tried flagging down the occasional car that passed by but we were on a country road and there was no one around who could help - until the coach came along. As soon as they spotted us, they stopped to see what was the problem. It was no problem to them; the coach had a pump. As one of the young men began to pump up the tyre the choir gathered around him and encouraged him by singing, in time to his pumping, the Chorus of the Hebrew Slaves from Verdi's opera *Nabucco*! That task completed, about 10 of the men **lifted** the jeep, while the faulty tyre was removed and the spare fitted. Everyone then climbed back into their respective vehicles and we continued on our way. By the time we reached Ploieşti it was late evening. We were grateful for a drink and a meal and to be able to collapse into bed. It had been quite a day!

Our timetable was taken over in the nicest possible way by Rebeca, a lady whose gentle manner hid a streak of determination. She insisted the next day was for relaxation so arranged to take us to see another of Ceauşescu's villas and gave us the opportunity to relax with other church members. The day after that we would spend with Adriana's family.

At last the day arrived when we could really begin to get down to business with the family. Catalin came again to help with the interpretation. His English was superb and, as we were now alone with the family, with no other church visitors it was so much easier to talk to Olga, Faby and Adriana. We were able to piece together so much more of what had been happening and tell them what we hoped would happen. They were amazed and shook their heads in disbelief as they saw the newspaper cuttings we had taken with us and heard about the way in which so many people from all over the country had responded to the article in the *Baptist Times*. Adriana showed us a letter she had received that day from a young man in America. She couldn't understand who he was or why he was writing to her. I explained that he had read the *Baptist Times*, at home in Dallas, Texas, and had written to me to ask for more details and for the family's address - proof of the way the *Baptist Times* article had been used. They were astounded!

Olga, Faby, Catalin and I spent some considerable time in the bathroom while I took measurements and made sketches of where the bath, basin, toilet and pipes were, so that we could see if we could purchase any aids in England to make Adriana more independent. Adriana, who couldn't join us because her wheelchair was too wide, knocked on the door wanting to know what three ladies and a man were doing in the bathroom! We told her not to be so nosey! It was an important time because it gave us an opportunity to talk more freely about what was needed.

Eventually, Catalin went to join the men while we ladies went into the bedroom to perform the more delicate task of taking photographs of Adriana's stumps. She was extremely co-operative and very patient, even though we had to converse mainly in sign language. I was grateful that she made it so easy for me, although I realised it couldn't have been easy for her. She showed me the book of physiotherapy exercises which Grace had sent and assured me she was doing some of them. I encouraged her to keep at it as these exercises were most important.

Later Rebeca and some of the church folk came to say goodbye, as we were leaving next morning. Catalin left, as he had not seen his family since breakfast but Vasile's friend, Nic, arrived, so we were not bereft of an interpreter. After chatting for a while Nic produced his guitar and we all sang. I asked Adriana if she played the guitar. No - but she had played the mandolin before the accident. Why not now? They looked puzzled. "Wasn't it obvious?" was the unspoken question. Undeterred, we asked "Would she play it for us now? We don't often hear the mandolin in our churches." "Oh no! That's not possible because it is out of tune," was the reply. Nic came to the rescue. "I can tune it for you," he said. Now there was no excuse. It was duly tuned and Adriana played it while we all sang. She was a bit rusty but at least was beginning to realise that the accident did not mean the end of all useful life. We enthused about how well she played and told her to practise every day and bring the mandolin with her when she came to England. She looked surprised, but agreed when we said it would be a great treat for us to hear her play it: one small victory!

The following morning we left Ploieşti to rejoin our party at Poiana Braşov, ready for the long haul by coach to Mamaia and the plane for England. Olga and Peter, Vasile, Faby and Nic came to see us off. It was the first time Olga had been back to the railway station since Adriana's accident. She and Faby left the rest of us chatting and slowly walked the length of the platform deep in conversation. I saw them pointing at the track, then they turned and beckoned to us. As we walked towards them Nic said quietly, "This is the platform where Adriana had her accident". It was easy to see how it had happened. Stepping off the platform on to the track is like stepping off a kerb on to a road; they are almost the same level. Adriana would have had no chance to correct her balance before she was pulled under the wheels. It didn't bear thinking about!

As we boarded our train there were more tears from Olga as she hugged us. We left with the assurance in our hearts that it had been right for us to come - and just an inkling of the enormous task ahead of us.

10: The ball is rolling!

On our return from Romania, we found a huge amount of post waiting for us including some cheques from readers of The Limbless Association magazine *Step Forward*. Further down the pile we found a copy of the September issue of the magazine. Our appeal letter had been printed. Wonderful!

Now that we had seen the situation first-hand, we realised that a lot of decisions would soon need to be taken and it was important that more of our church members should become involved in the planning arrangements. A small committee was needed. Sheila Cutler and Anne Pitkethly had a little knowledge of Romania from their lorry trip. Grace Miller had been involved from the beginning and her medical experience would be invaluable. No official nominations were necessary - the committee really formed itself. All three were more than willing to take on the extra load and to meet as regularly as possible for prayer and planning sessions.

The first task was to report back to our surgeon friend, Geoff, following our visit to Adriana and see what he suggested our next move should be. He said that, from the photographs, her stumps appeared to be quite good and probably the next step would be to get an opinion from a specialist limbfitter. He suggested I wrote to the Disablement Services Centre at Oxford. They had already provided a new leg for Maria and another Romanian girl only a month or so earlier, so we were not too optimistic that they would be able to take on another case so soon but I wrote anyway and sent copies of the photographs we had taken of Adriana's stumps.

A week or so later we had our first big setback. The Oxford Centre could not take on the job. The two previous amputees they had helped were already established limb wearers and just needed better replacements. Adriana's problem was much greater as she needed a full rehabilitation package which would require either in-patient or regular out-patient treatment plus a lot of input from the limbfitters.

My heart sank as I read on: "There will also be long-term problems associated with supplying her with a pair of artificial limbs, because in this type of situation, limb fitting is by no means a one-off exercise. Certainly, her amputation stumps will be likely to change in volume so that she would in time require new sockets for her artificial limbs (which is also a costly and time-consuming exercise), and it is evident from the

Romanian amputees whom we have already seen, that facilities for adjusting and maintaining artificial limbs in Romania are minimal. It might be therefore, that even if she did obtain good initial function with a pair of artificial limbs, she would not be able to maintain this in the long term once back at home. If she were admitted either here or in Milton Keynes for a prolonged period of rehabilitation, this would be likely to cost considerably more than your budget allows ...

... It would certainly be possible to provide Miss Dobre with a pair of artificial limbs, but there must be a great deal of uncertainty about the long-term usefulness of such a programme in her case. The 39 steps to her apartment might prove an insuperable barrier, even if she did have a pair of artificial limbs."

That was a blow we had not foreseen. I telephoned Oxford and had a long and frank discussion with the specialist. He told me that if there were any of the problems they envisaged, we could well be looking at a total cost of nearer £20,000. This was certainly not the kind of news we had hoped to hear! By now our church was becoming really geared up to the thought that we were getting nearer to bringing Adriana to England, especially as it was obvious that it was a much more urgent matter than we had originally thought. Money was still coming in by every post and from various efforts among the church members. We were well on the way to our initial target but £20,000 was a little different! Although the whole matter needed much prayer and wisdom I did not feel that this was the kind of news that should be made public at this stage. Instead I shared it with the committee. We came to the conclusion that our burden had been to give Adriana the opportunity to walk again. We must press ahead with that aim. What happened after that was up to the limbfitters, Adriana and the Lord who had given us the task to do. Surely He would not give us such a task if it was doomed to failure?

That decision made, we went ahead with our planning. By the end of my telephone conversation with Oxford we had come to the conclusion that the best thing to do was to contact Otto Bock again. So I wrote to Olaf Boyle, sending further copies of the photographs. Within days he called me. "When is she coming to England?" he asked. I mentioned that we thought we might have to wait until she had stopped growing.

"That will be too late," he said. "In fact, it might already be too late for her to walk properly again. She needs to come as soon as possible."

He agreed with most of the assessment we had just had but said there was a possibility, as she was only 16, that she could adapt more quickly. He said that the stumps looked good, although there was a lot of swelling which would shrink quite quickly once the legs were fitted and being used.

Rehabilitation was possible but there were still many more questions to be asked, which he patiently answered. I asked what would it entail and he said we would need an initial visit to the limbfitter, followed by about a ten-day stay while the legs were made and fitted. Then Adriana would need walking training about three times a week minimum.

I asked where she could have this treatment and was told that Roehampton was a possibility or the Otto Bock facilities at Egham in Surrey. What sort of time scale were we looking at? Six weeks? Three months? He could not give me the answer to that until Adriana had been examined.

Along with the revived hope came a host of other problems. Where would they stay while the initial process was taking place? How would we manage physio sessions three times a week at such a distance? Should we try to enlist the help of another church in the area of the limbfitters? How could we ask someone else to take on a task that we felt we had been given? By now there was a real sense of love for this family whom most of our members had never met, a real prayer concern for Adriana, and a tremendous enthusiasm as everyone did their own little bit to help.

We had received a letter from Adriana saying, "When I come to your country I shall have to come with my mother as I can not travel alone". We already knew that. It was obvious to all of us that, when Adriana came, her mother would have to accompany her. We might need Olga's consent for surgery or other decisions which might need to be taken. It was not right for Adriana to come alone.

That in turn raised another problem - neither Adriana nor Olga spoke English. It would be necessary to provide an interpreter. How could we ask another church to have the same commitment to take this on, with all the unanswered questions? It didn't feel right to do that.

Whatever details were to be worked out, the most important one right now was to get the documents together to issue the necessary official invitation to Adriana and her mother to come to England, so that they could start applying for their passports and visas. Geoff supplied us with an official medical letter saying it was imperative that Adriana should come for treatment; I wrote a letter on behalf of the church promising that they would come as our guests and we would provide all accommodation and food and also we would pay for all medical services. We gathered together as many important-looking documents as we could in the hope that the officially headed notepaper would impress the authorities at the other end! These were all to be sent to Olga via one of the travellers from RomAF. They were far too precious to trust to the vagaries of the Romanian postal service! Copies of all the documents were also sent to the British Embassy in Bucharest and the Home Office in London. We wanted to make sure everyone knew so that no one should put any blocks in the way.

In the meantime I wrote to Olga telling her what was happening and asking if there was any possibility of them finding an interpreter to come with them. This seemed the logical solution. We might be able to find someone locally in Milton Keynes who could speak some Romanian but how could we expect that person to be available all the time? We might even find several Romanian speakers. In that case there would be the problem of arranging rotas. What would happen if something unexpected turned up and the interpreter was unable to come just at a critical time? What would happen if Adriana or her mother needed any counselling or help and there was no one available to help us? We were certain that they needed to have a native Romanian speaker with them.

Already such a situation had arisen right here in Milton Keynes, just a month or so earlier, with a Romanian who had come to England for surgery but could not speak English and had no one who could interpret for him. Valerie at RomAF had been involved in the many problems this situation caused and we had learned a valuable lesson from the experience. There was no doubt in our minds that we needed a full-time interpreter.

It seemed best for Adriana's family to find someone who would be willing to come with them and stay with them all the time. We did not want them to feel isolated through language difficulties. But there were also other requirements for our interpreter, so these had to be spelt out in my letter to Olga.

"It needs to be someone who would be willing and able to give possibly up to six weeks of their time to being with you morning till night, at home, with the doctor, with the physiotherapist, with your hosts, etc.

It needs to be someone whom Adriana would be happy to have with her when she is being examined by doctors or working with the physiotherapist, as we don't want to cause her any embarrassment (in other words, the interpreter would have to be female).

It needs to be someone with a fairly good command of English who will realise that this is not the opportunity for a free holiday, but hard work."

This was expecting the impossible - but William Carey, the founder of the Baptist Missionary Society, once said, "Attempt great things for God - expect great things from God." We had entered into this commitment sure that it was a God-given task. We had to believe He had the answers to all the problems.

By this time, four months into our appeal, it was mid-September. Now we just stood back and watched in amazement as, within a period of three or four days, the whole operation was taken out of our hands.

First, I had a telephone call - from Bob Watts, the Managing Director of Dorset Orthopaedic, a firm of limb-fitters at St Leonard's Hospital, Ringwood, Hampshire. He had read our appeal letter in The Limbless Association magazine. "How is the fund going?" he asked. By now we felt we were in reach of our initial target - although a long way short of what might be needed. "I would like to make you an offer," he said. "I am willing to make and fit limbs for this young lady, free of charge." Just like that! I was, for once, at a loss for words! He went on to ask further questions, which I answered on auto-pilot as I tried to take in what he was offering and all the implications at this end. I explained that we were already in touch with Otto Bock and he said, "That is no problem. I use Otto Bock components". It was all too much - I thanked him very much for his offer - and said I would let him know! I needed time to collect my thoughts!

Needless to say, our telephone line was humming that evening as all the committee were consulted. I also rang Geoff Miller, who immediately said, "Go for it!" I felt I had been rather ungracious in not accepting Bob's offer immediately - but it raised all sorts of similar problems to the ones we already were working through with Otto Bock. Ringwood is also a long way from Milton Keynes.

The very next day I had another call. "George Buckley here. Does the name ring a bell?" Only a very faint one! Where had I heard that name before? Another clue was needed and it came, "Romania!" That much I had already guessed as there was hardly a phone call now that did not relate to Romania in some way. He asked, "Did you see the TV programme on BBC last week, called *Children of the Castle.*" Then the penny dropped. I **had** seen the programme. "Oh! You're the MENCAP man," I spluttered. Yes, he was the MENCAP man who had been featured on the heart-rending programme about the plight of the Romanian orphans. A retired headmaster of a school for the mentally handicapped, he had been so moved by the plight of the orphans that he had gone out to Romania with a team from the Bristol branch of MENCAP and was actively helping to renovate this 'Hospital for Irrecuperables' at Brincovenești near Tirgu Mureș in the middle of Romania.

George continued, "What they didn't show on the film was that I have an artificial leg!" By now I was speechless - what was coming next? I didn't have long to wait. "I read your appeal in The Limbless Association magazine. I was in Dorset Orthopaedic yesterday having adjustments made to my leg and Bob Watts told me about his offer to you. I am just ringing to let you know that, if you decide to accept there is no need to worry about accommodation or meals. I can arrange that through our local Rotary Club or one of the local churches." I put down the telephone, almost in tears. Why were we worrying over things like interpreters and visas and long distance visits to physio sessions? Who was actually in charge of this project? I sat down and wrote a letter to Bob Watts accepting his offer! The rest would fall into place. By now, I had no doubts at all about that.

Geoff and Grace agreed to try to find a physiotherapist locally who could take on Adriana's walking training, while I wrote to Otto Bock telling them all the latest developments and that we were taking up Bob's offer. I asked them to forward the photographs and other details to Bob.

October 15th 1990 was the day when everything happened at once! First, Roy answered the phone. It was George, wanting to speak to me. "Are you a member of her staff?" he asked! Roy reckoned that, by this time, that just about summed up the situation! It seemed to us that the telephone had hardly ever stopped ringing since we returned from Romania and almost all the calls seemed to be for me. When I reached the 'phone, George told me that everything was arranged. The Coach House Hotel near St Leonard's Hospital had offered us free accommodation, leaving only the meals to pay for! "But don't worry about that," continued George, "because the local Rotary Club has agreed to cover those!" This was unbelievable! "But do they realise there will be four of us?" I replied. "Adriana and her mother, plus an interpreter and me." "That's no problem," he said. "Just let me know when you're coming and I'll make all the necessary arrangements."

It was time to really start moving. We were told that the visas should take about six weeks to process, so we were obviously looking at this side of Christmas for their arrival.

Later Geoff 'phoned. "I have found you a physiotherapist!" "Where?" I asked cautiously. "Right here in Milton Keynes," he replied. That was marvellous news. The person he had spoken to was Ann Dring, the Senior Physiotherapist for Amputees in the area. She had agreed to take on the challenge of Adriana and hoped to be able to do it at The Saxon Clinic, the local private hospital. She needed clearance from the authorities and other physiotherapists there first.

Next, Valerie rang from the RomAF office. An interpreter had been found through the Baptist pastor in Sibiu but she could only come for two or three weeks. That was a start so we accepted the offer gratefully. The family in Ploieşti could only find a male English teacher, who wasn't suitable bearing in mind the very intimate help that Adriana would require.

It was not all good news. Olaf Boyle rang to say that our willingness to take up Bob Watts's offer at Dorset Orthopaedic was very understandable but warned me that he felt Bob might need to modify his offer as Adriana's stumps would begin to shrink very quickly once she was walking and she could need several changes of socket before returning to Romania. That could be a costly business. The whole thing was not by any means as straightforward as it sounded. Sometimes it felt as though we were going two steps forward and one step back.

Later, I contacted Ann Dring, the physiotherapist. Everything was arranged. Everyone was happy for her to do the physiotherapy on a private basis and The Saxon Clinic had offered their gym facilities free of charge!

We had now reached the stage where, rather than initiating contacts, I was sitting back and waiting for the next telephone call. We had been 'taken over' and there was no doubt in our minds, as all this was reported to the church meeting, that the Lord was very definitely in control of this project.

11: Down to details

It was only one month since we had returned from our visit to Romania but events were moving very quickly. Now that the medical arrangements were fixed up, we could concentrate more on what was needed at the Romanian end. The family still could not find anyone suitable who was able to spare all the time needed to come and act as interpreter. We had to accept the offer of the young lady in Sibiu (another Adriana, we were told) and believe that someone else would be provided when the time came for her to return home.

David Milborrow, who was at that time a member of the RomAF Committee, was visiting Sibiu and arranged to provide the interpreter with the necessary invitation documents plus the money for the plane tickets. Once all the passports had been obtained it was necessary for Olga and the interpreter, Addy, to travel to Bucharest for visas. Their first visit to the Embassy was scheduled for 22nd October and Pastor Ioan accompanied Olga.

Also in October, Grace and I visited a large exhibition of aids for the disabled at Alexandra Palace to see what was available. We were looking specifically for bath aids as we felt it was important that Adriana should become independent in this area as soon as possible. We came away with bags bulging with catalogues and leaflets about things which just might prove to be useful in the future.

Our committee met again to work out some sort of schedule for our visitors arrival. We could plan as far as the initial consultation with the limbfitters but then had to work out two different strategies depending on what was decided about the need for further surgery. It was also necessary to work out hospitality for our three guests. We had had a number of offers of beds and/or meals and had to decide on the priorities.

It was essential that any home where Adriana stayed should have a downstairs toilet which automatically ruled out some of the offers. It was not going to be easy finding someone who could accommodate all three of our guests. It was also important for the interpreter that she should be given some time to herself. Therefore it seemed best to put Olga and Adriana in one home and the interpreter in another - reasonably near each other if possible.

We felt we needed to offer a few guidelines to those who had offered hospitality of any kind which we could all follow in order to try and make our visitors' stay here as happy and productive as possible. As we felt it was important that all the host families had a common policy, I drafted some notes on 'Hospitality for our Romanian Visitors' which we gave to prospective hosts.

Some of the things mentioned seemed very basic but we had learned a lot in the RomAF office about Romanians coming to England and it was good to be able to draw on that experience and try to avoid possible trouble spots. We did not want any embarrassing situations to arise on either side.

The notes highlighted the fact that one potential problem could be that of expectation. For our church to be able to afford to fly Olga, Adriana and the interpreter to England, as well as provide hospitality and artificial legs, could make us seem like millionaires in Romanian eyes. They had no idea what to expect when they arrived. Olga had already asked in a letter, "When I come, will I need to bring clothes?" We wanted to show tender loving care - but not to pamper them and shower them with gifts. This had been done with many who came from their country to ours - with devastating results in some cases. We knew of cases where Romanians exposed too quickly to the abundance of the West had actually had breakdowns. We could not afford to take the risk of anything like that happening. We also had to remember that they would have to return to the conditions in Romania eventually and we did not want to do anything that might make that more difficult for them. Bearing in mind the terrible oppression which they had had to endure for so long and the chronic shortages of all basic necessities they were still facing, it was only natural that people would want to show their love and concern through gifts, but that could be counter-productive.

Food was another area where problems could arise. This could have been a bit sensitive. Most housewives are used to entertaining visitors and might wonder who on earth we thought we were, telling them what to serve their guests! However it was necessary to make the hostesses aware that the normal, everyday meal in Romanian homes was watery vegetable soup accompanied by lots of bread, with tomatoes, cheese and salami when they were available and occasionally meat and potatoes (both of which were rationed). Fresh fruit such as bananas or oranges were unobtainable luxuries in Romania. Fresh cream trifle or chocolate gâteau might be a nice treat today, but if tomorrow's hostess provided the same, our guests could be in for some digestive upsets! Also, it was important that Adriana did not put on weight because that would affect her stumps and her walking ability.

We had to bear in mind that this was a new country, strange language and very different culture. Several Romanians over here had said to us: "It is another world" and that is difficult to understand unless you have seen their world. A short trip to the local supermarket could be mind-blowing for them. The huge shopping centre in Milton Keynes should therefore be a no-go area for a little while until they had adapted.

We could have upset our members by setting out such elementary ground rules but none of us had had visitors quite like these before. We had to make their introduction to the wealthy and super-abundant West as gentle as possible. We were grateful that all the hostesses accepted the reasons behind the few tips offered and realised that we were drawing on the experience of others to try to avoid some of the problems that had arisen. We had enough problems of a different kind coming up!

By now we were all concerned that Adriana was spending too much of her time at home just sitting watching TV. Although we had suggested that Olga should try to structure her day and make sure the exercises were done regularly, every week's delay could make it more difficult for her eventual rehabilitation as her hips could set. We dare not delay any more. Bob had written to confirm that he would make and fit Adriana's legs free of any charge but we would have to pay for the Otto Bock components. We were extremely grateful to him. Gradually the £20,000 estimate was being reduced to more manageable proportions!

Obviously, Adriana was going to need a wheelchair while she was here. We impressed on Vasile the need to mention, when he booked the ticket, that Adriana would need assistance at the airport. In fact, taking note of an article written by a disabled girl in The Limbless Association magazine, who had had some very unpleasant experiences when travelling by air, we suggested they should mention it when he booked the ticket, when they arrived at the airport and at passport control. Once on board the aircraft they should check with the stewardess that the news had been radioed on ahead by the captain. In other words they should nag them until they were sure it was happening! It was not going to be a very pleasant experience for Adriana being manhandled up and down the aircraft steps and we wanted to make sure that she and Olga were not left in the lurch. As far as this end was concerned, I rang Heathrow to make sure there would be a wheelchair available. I might as well have tried to contact Mars - (or Bucharest!). However, after I had been passed on to other numbers seven times, I hit the jackpot! A helpful young man told me all I needed to know. Now, once we were armed with the date of the flight, we were in business!

On 23rd October we had another telephone call from Nic. The visas had been applied for and would be ready in two or three days. Olga would return to the Embassy to collect them. He suggested that Olga and

Adriana should come when they could and the interpreter could come when her visa was available. Alarm bells rang! They must all travel together on the same plane on the same day. Nothing else was acceptable. There was no way we could manage extra journeys to Heathrow or the initial settling in period without the interpreter. She was absolutely integral to everything working smoothly - and we still had one for only three weeks.

There were still many arrangements to be made. Anne arranged to borrow an ambulance from the Red Cross so that we could all travel in one vehicle to and from Heathrow. Meanwhile, Ken was trying to establish contact with another double amputee we had heard about in our area as we felt it would be useful for Adriana to meet someone near her own age with a similar disability as early as possible.

By 29th October, we had still not heard if the visas had been obtained. I tried to 'phone Nic and several others but lines to Romania were unobtainable. In desperation I rang the International Operator and explained the problem. He was most helpful and kept on trying every ten minutes for two hours. Eventually he got through - to an operator in Prague in Czechoslovakia who told him "Romania and Poland - very difficult!" You can say that again! Eventually, I gave up.

A visit to my father in Burnley was long overdue. As there was no apparent movement on the visa front, it was decided that it was 'now or never'. So I disappeared for three days. Just before leaving, I heard that the visas had been granted and would be collected on Friday, 2nd November. Once again, RomAF travellers, this time from Banbury, happened to be in the right place at the right time. They were able to help with the formalities at the Embassy in Bucharest and forged links that were to be strengthened later when Adriana was here.

Life was becoming really frenetic! The Limbless Association asked me to write an article for the December issue of their magazine; the *Baptist Times* was keeping in close touch with what was happening and keeping Adriana in the public eye as far as their readership was concerned, so letters and cheques were still arriving by every post; Radio Bedford interviews were becoming a regular part of life. Every spare minute was spent either writing letters or on the telephone. Normal jobs were relegated to the 'pending' file and convenience foods became essential commodities - if we wanted to eat!

Also, since the revolution in December 1989, the work at the RomAF office had increased dramatically and more help was needed to keep abreast with all the correspondence which was flooding in. The directors asked me if I would be willing to increase my hours in the office. There was no doubt in my mind as I accepted their offer and handed in my resignation to my headteacher at the school. Romania and her people were now very dear to my heart and I was delighted to have the opportunity to become more involved. My one day a week at RomAF increased to three.

At midnight on 7th November, Nic rang. The visas and tickets had been collected and all three would be arriving at Heathrow Airport on Sunday 11th November at 11.30am. The moment we had been working for had almost arrived!

Once the date came through I had a checklist of seventeen jobs to go through, so the next day was 'telephone day'. Adriana's appointment for assessment at Ringwood had to be booked, plus accommodation, not to mention transport to and from Dorset. The committee and the hostess for the interpreter had to be mobilised. The surgeon, physiotherapist and other interested parties such as the *Baptist Times* and Radio Bedford needed to be notified of her imminent arrival.

In order to avoid too many changes of home for our guests but to give the hostesses a break, it was decided that they should stay at the manse for the first few weeks, then move on to Anne and Sheila for subsequent months. It seemed an obvious choice as Adriana and her mother had met us before and therefore we would be two familiar faces among a sea of unknowns. Doris Couper, who lived nearby, agreed to take the interpreter. We had suggested that Olga should come for a week or so to see Adriana settled in and, once her legs had been fitted and the walking training commenced, she could go back to Romania to be with her family in time for Christmas. If necessary, she could return at a later date to take Adriana home. Accordingly we had told her to apply for a double-entry visa, valid for six months. We were to discover later that she had made up her mind that there was no way she was going home. She had looked after the family for plenty of Christmasses - this year they could look after themselves! Olga was going to spend **her** Christmas in England!

A notice went up on our ROMANIA notice board in church with a programme for each day and the sort of help needed. A column left blank for offers of help was rapidly filled up by church folk offering transport, meals, 'phone-sitting, or whatever else was required.

On the morning of Sunday 11th November 1990, Ken collected the ambulance from the Red Cross and set off with Anne, Sheila, Peter and me for Heathrow Airport Terminal 2 to meet flight RO209 from Bucharest. All the preparations were behind us. The day we had been working for had arrived. We had no idea of what lay ahead of us. All we knew was that the Lord who had guided us through all the yesterdays would see us through today and also take care of all the tomorrows.

12: Settling in

After an interminable wait in the arrivals hall at Heathrow, at last we saw Adriana in a wheelchair, being pushed by a member of British Airways staff. They were closely followed by a huge pile of luggage on a trolley, on top of which, to our delight, was a bag which obviously contained a mandolin. Olga, who was guiding the trolley and was almost hidden behind it, beamed and waved as she spotted us in the crowd. Walking with her and helping to control the trolley was a taller, thin-faced young woman with black shoulder-length hair who we presumed was our interpreter. She held out her hand in greeting as we ducked under the rope barrier to take charge of the luggage. "Hello! I am Adriana," she said and was soon in business as all the introductions got under way. One of the first details to sort out was what we should call her. "Call me Addy," she said. "Two Adrianas would be too confusing."

The luggage was loaded into the ambulance, Adriana was lifted in, and soon we were on our way along the M25 and M1 towards Milton Keynes. There was a lot of chatter at the front of the vehicle between Anne, Sheila and Addy. Adriana spent most of the journey just looking out of the window, chewing gum, while Olga and I sat quietly in the back, just holding hands. There was little need for words. She was very possessive of one of her bags of luggage and would not let anyone else handle it. It contained, she told us, fragile things. We were to discover treasures galore when that bag was opened. Out of it during the next few months, came a seemingly endless supply of gifts. Everyone who helped in any way found themselves recipients of something from Romania.

The rehabilitation process started immediately for Adriana when we arrived home and I pointed out the downstairs toilet. It was very small but I had previously practised getting in, closing the door and getting out again, in a wheelchair, so I knew it could be done. As we were to discover so many times during the next few months, Adriana thought it was impossible. I insisted that she tried. She did - and she managed it. It wasn't easy, but she succeeded, one small step, but such an important one on the long road to independence and complete rehabilitation. Disabled people in Romania are regarded as useless and soon begin to regard themselves in that light. If something looks impossible then it is impossible, so there's no point in trying. Adriana had to start to regain some confidence in her ability to do the small things before she could attempt the bigger ones - and there was no time to lose.

Our church-owned manse is an average-sized three-bedroomed detached house - nothing elaborate, furnished in the way manses often are, with much of the furniture having seen better days. To us it is home, a place where we feel comfortable. To Olga and Adriana it was a palace. I showed Olga into the guest room where she would sleep. When she saw the double bed she automatically assumed it was for Adriana and herself to share. "No," I said, "Adriana will be in here", pointing to the smaller spare room which doubles as my study. Olga wanted to know where Addy would sleep and when told she would be in another home nearby, indicated that Addy could sleep in the bed designated for Adriana and she and Adriana would sleep together. "No," I said again, "You will both need some privacy and space to yourselves during the weeks ahead. You will have a room each and Addy will come here each day." Olga just could not believe that she would have a bed all to herself - it was a luxury she had never dreamed of. At home in Ploieşti there are three bedrooms in their apartment. Every room has at least two people sleeping there and sometimes more. You are never sure when going to sleep if you will wake up with the same number of people in the bed, as Bibi, the youngest son, often wakes in the night and decides to change beds.

Olga walked around the house exclaiming at the space, marvelling at my elderly electric cooker, admiring the wallpaper, and becoming almost ecstatic when she saw the bathroom, which, for some reason has more space than the kitchen! To her it was all **foarte frumos** (very beautiful).

The next test came that first evening, when it was time for bed. I turned to see Olga struggling to carry Adriana up the stairs in her arms. "No," I exclaimed, "You mustn't do that. She must go up by herself." They looked completely astounded! There it was again - that attitude of "She can't do that, don't you realise she has no legs?" "Tomorrow, I'll show you," I promised. "We do not want Olga to end up with a strained back."

The following evening I made sure I was around when it was time to go upstairs and showed Adriana how to sit on the stairs and pull herself up by using her hands and the bannister rail. I'd practised that too. She got halfway and collapsed in a heap saying, "I can't!" Olga was on her way to pick her up when I stopped her. "Yes, you can. Rest for a moment, then try again." It was almost as exhausting to stand and watch as it was for Adriana to heave herself up but we had to be firm. Eventually she got to the top amid great praise from everyone! Two new things achieved in two days - that wasn't bad. Within a week Adriana was going upstairs on her bottom as though she'd been doing it for years.

The timetable on the church notice board was soon filled up as our church folk were eager to come to welcome them to England and to wish

Adriana well. It was hard work for Addy, interpreting. She had arrived feeling very unwell, with an extremely heavy cold, so we tried to keep the mornings quiet so that she could have time to rest and recover. Olga would happily sit in her bedroom, singing or reading her Bible. Adriana, like any teenager, enjoyed lying in bed in the morning, so everyone was happy. I could go off to work, leaving some soup and a pile of sandwiches for lunch and Roy could work in the study - until they came down late morning for breakfast.

There were several important things to fit in during the first week. First and foremost, Adriana and her mother had to see what artificial legs would look like. They had no idea what to expect. Adriana told me much later that she had expected wooden legs, painted flesh colour! We arranged for two young ladies to visit, one who was an amputee and the other who had been born without legs, so had never walked normally. The visit was useful as they were able to demonstrate how the legs were put on and taken off. Olga, Adriana and Addy were able to see and feel them. We only found out much later how dismayed Adriana had been when she had seen how one of the girls lurched when walking. She determined that, if she walked again, she would not lurch. But that was a long way in the future.

Another immediate requirement was a visit from Ann, the physiotherapist. She came to our house one evening to assess Adriana's mobility and they both did exercises on the floor. She was very pleased with the flexibility of Adriana's hip joints. Obviously the exercises she had been doing from the book Grace had sent had proved beneficial. That was one hurdle over. The next step was the appointment with the limbfitter for his assessment of whether further surgery would be needed. We were all hopeful now that it would not be necessary.

On the suggestion of Geoff, the surgeon, we had bought the video *Reach for the Sky*, the story of Group Captain Douglas Bader, the flying ace who lost both legs. Although it is an old black-and-white film, it graphically portrays his struggles and his determination to succeed. It would give Adriana an idea of what is possible, even for a double amputee, as well as a foretaste of all the hard work ahead of her. We learned much later that this film had greatly encouraged her.

The telephone never stopped ringing that first week. Radio Bedford was anxious to interview Adriana, so Barry Amis came one afternoon with his tape recorder. Several of our church young people were here too, so it made for a lively interview. One of the local papers rang for another interview and another amputee offered to come and talk to Adriana.

Inevitably there were difficulties to overcome and cultural differences to come to terms with. Adriana had been used to watching the TV whenever she wanted. She soon learned how to work the remote control switch on our set and it became quite a battle sometimes to turn it off in the middle of a programme when more visitors arrived. It was often used as a smoke screen to hide behind when she'd had enough of being talked to. She also discovered very quickly how to read the TV programmes in the daily paper - and memorised the times of the films on the different channels! Immediately a meal was over she would wheel herself into the lounge and switch on. By the time we got there she could be well into a film. Sometimes Olga would be there with her, with Addy sitting between them, translating. When friends lent her several video recordings of well-known films and she wanted to watch them in one day we realised that it was a bit of an addiction and one of our first aims must be to wean her away from reliance on the TV.

We soon got used to serving dinner accompanied by a huge plateful of bread. Occasionally I would forget or think it was not necessary with a particular meal, but was always reminded that it was missing! I had never seen bread disappear so quickly and in such quantities! Satsumas and bananas were very quickly established as firm favourites and also disappeared at an alarming rate. It didn't take long to discover why - they would sit and watch a TV film with a bowl full in front of them and steadily munch their way through the lot! Apples weren't touched - "We have those at home," we were told! They thought our habit of offering all visitors a cup of tea was very strange. They didn't drink so often at home, they told us.

At mealtimes, Olga would try anything, as long as it was accompanied by piles of bread! Adriana was a typical 16-year-old who would refuse boiled potatoes on the ground that they were fattening, then eat a whole bag of potato crisps without a second thought. Getting rid of the chewing gum long enough to eat the meal was a major triumph - it was often stuck under the plate, only to reappear as soon as the meal was finished. (I never did find out how she got her supplies.) Addy would say "Just a little - then I will come back for more" - and she usually did!

Conversation was not always easy. One of us might ask a question of Olga, which would be interpreted by Addy. We soon learned that Olga tended to speak in 'paragraphs' or even 'chapters', never a simple sentence. As we waited with bated breath for Addy's translation of a long explanation, it would come in one simple sentence. It was no doubt a very accurate summing-up by Addy of what Olga had said, but usually it put an end to that particular conversation. If we pressed for more, particularly at the meal-table, it meant that Addy had to allow her meal to go cold while she interpreted the conversation for both parties. Later, we learned that Addy had been told before coming that an interpreter's job was to interpret what was said, not to translate every word. It was often very frustrating. Adriana said very little, except to occasionally chip in to her mother's conversation with apparently differing views.

Every outing became a major operation and preparations had to be started in good time with three of them to get ready. They had to be told well in advance what time we were going, so they did not become immersed in a film or another TV programme. If that happened, it blew the whole timetable to smithereens as we were told "Just a minute, until we see . . ." When all three were ready, Adriana had to be helped into the front seat of the car and the wheelchair put in the boot, before everyone else climbed in. Once we reached our destination the procedure was reversed.

A sense of humour was a great asset when things got a bit trying! They had to get used to our habits too. For example, we did not wear anything on our heads to go out in the November weather, whereas Olga wore her hat and her boots indoors and outdoors, all day long. I was in trouble with Olga for going out clad in a short wool jacket and no boots! Everything was strange for all of us and allowances had to be made.

It was only a few days before other problems began to surface. We had suggested that Olga brought something to keep her busy as, after coping with such a large family at home, there was the distinct possibility she could become bored - another reason for watching TV so much we presumed. I knew she had brought her macramé and one day asked why she was not doing it. She told me that her spectacles were so old that she could not see even to read her Bible properly. Something obviously had to be done about that, so we made an appointment with an optician. Ten days later she was the proud possessor of two new pairs of spectacles, one for close work and the other for distance. She was like a woman reborn! What was more - when the optician realised she was from Romania he provided one pair of frames free of charge! That was the kind of generosity we were finding wherever we turned.

Then Addy announced that she thought she was probably pregnant! She had only been married six months before she volunteered to come and help us. Her husband was a student in the Baptist Seminary in Bucharest. As her heavy cold improved, the morning sickness started! It seemed a good idea to make an appointment for an ante-natal check before she went back to Romania.

Before we knew it a week had passed and it was Sunday again. Needless to say, our three visitors received a great welcome at church. In fact, most of the congregation had already called at the manse during the week to meet them and some had already had them in their homes.

Sunday was also the day we were to travel to Ringwood for the first appointment with the limbfitter. We left Bletchley on Sunday afternoon and had only gone a few miles when Addy beseeched Dave Griffin, who was driving, to stop the car. He stopped and she got out quickly and was promptly sick on the grass verge. When she had recovered enough to get back into the car, she informed us that she was always travel-sick in a car! I groaned inwardly as I thought of the number of 240-mile round trips to Ringwood we were likely to be making in the next few weeks.

Dave returned to Bletchley to report that we had all arrived safely, while Adriana, Olga, Addy and I stayed overnight at the hotel in Ringwood so that we would be ready by 9am on the Monday morning for a full day's session at the hospital. At last we felt something was going to happen about Adriana's legs.

13: New experiences

On our arrival at The Coach House Hotel, we were welcomed by members of both the Ferndown and Parkstone Rotary Clubs. George Buckley, who had made all the accommodation arrangements, was also there. It was good to meet him at last after all he had done for us. George stayed to have a meal with us in the restaurant. That was quite an experience for all of us. Everything on the menu had to be explained to our visitors in detail. The idea of pork chop with **peaches** was regarded with total horror by all three. They eventually opted for the chop but the waiter was told firmly, "No peaches!" I decided on chicken in sauce. When the meal was served it was examined very closely. Addy obviously decided she liked the look of mine better than hers. Reaching across the table with a spoon in her hand, she said "I'll have some of your sauce" as she helped herself to what was on my plate.

George arrived again early on Monday morning to take us to St Leonard's Hospital. He had taken us completely under his wing and we were being thoroughly spoiled. Once we arrived at the clinic, where George was obviously very well known, we met Bob Watts, Managing Director of Dorset Orthopaedic. After examining Adriana, Bob agreed that no further surgery seemed to be necessary and whisked her away to take plaster casts of her stumps. Addy accompanied them to interpret. There was no room in the small plaster room for any more people so Olga and I sat in the waiting room watching the other patients come and go. We watched, fascinated, as some patients turned up in wheelchairs with their artificial limbs across their knees and people in white coats walked in and out carrying legs and half-legs under their arms. We looked at the magazines available and I pointed out pictures on the wall of amputees playing basketball. Olga shook her head as though it was just too much to take in. We were unable to communicate much verbally but an occasional squeeze of the hand, a smile and a thumbs-up sign was all that was needed. Her mind was in that little room down the corridor and what was happening there. Eventually Adriana and Addy returned with Bob. The plaster casts had been taken successfully and we were invited to join him for lunch in the staff canteen.

It was just as well that we were a little late for lunch and there were few people left in the canteen. Although Adriana opted for a sandwich, the others had to be guided slowly past all the steaming hot trays of food, while I explained to Addy what each one was and she, in turn, translated for Olga. Once that had been done, we were back to which one to choose. Bob, who had led the way, watched his meal go cold on its plate as he patiently waited until everyone had been served with the meal of their choice. As we ate, we were joined by Bob's wife, Tessa, who worked as his secretary. They both asked a lot of questions about how we had become involved with Romania. They were a delightful couple; Bob, a quiet-spoken, fair-haired man with a ready smile, was somehow younger than I had imagined him from our conversations on the telephone. Tessa was very lively and friendly and I soon learned that they had two young daughters. They both had a tremendous interest in people. It was a very pleasant interlude but soon it was time for them to return to work.

Bob told us it would take a week for the stump sockets and legs to be made and then we would have to come back again for a fitting. Before that we would need to go out and buy Adriana a pair of shoes! That was music to the ears, but how does one buy shoes for someone with no legs? What size should we get? Is there a certain type which would be better than another? Bob had all the answers. Size five and a half, with a reasonably flat heel would do, he said. Turning to Adriana, he asked her, "How tall do you want to be? How tall were you before your accident?" After some discussion, working in metric and imperial measurements, 5ft 5in was decided upon. It was not quite as tall as she used to be but she had to be able to balance. The shorter she was and the larger the shoes she wore, the easier it would be to balance, but it all had to be in proportion. We couldn't have a girl of 4ft 6in in size 7 shoes!

We travelled home, tired but full of thankfulness. No further surgery was needed. We did not have to worry about leaving our friends to fend for themselves in a strange place as it could all be done from Bletchley. It would mean making quite a number of long journeys to Ringwood but that was a minor problem, apart from Addy's propensity to be travel-sick. However, on our return, I mentioned this to Grace and the next day she turned up with some wrist-bands which guaranteed to cure travel-sickness, among other things. Addy viewed them very sceptically but agreed to give them a try on our next trip. She was obviously certain they would not work but did not like to give offence by refusing them. To her amazement and my great relief, there was no more travel-sickness on any of our journeys.

Our next step now was to arrange a trip to the shops to purchase some new shoes. Progress was being made.

I was concerned about exposing them to the large, modern shopping centre in Central Milton Keynes before they'd had a chance to acclimatise slowly. It may have seemed over-cautious to some but through the contacts we had at the RomAF office we had heard some very worrying tales of the different reactions some Romanians had experienced when exposed suddenly to the abundance of goods in the shops here. The local parade of shops might be a better and more gentle introduction. So one afternoon having prepared them as well as I could, we walked up to the shops taking Adriana in the wheelchair. In the small supermarket, Addy and Adriana went down one aisle as Olga and I went down the other. Olga stopped in front of each shelf, stroking her hand gently across the front of the goods as she murmured, with a half-sigh "Ay, ay, ay". I gave her as much time as she wanted and eventually we reached the end of the shop where there was a small cooked meat stand, no more than 3 to 4 ft wide. Above that small refrigerated cabinet were hanging some packs of sliced meat and in the cabinet were two bacon joints. Suddenly Olga called urgently, "Adriana!" Addy came running and Adriana wheeled herself as quickly as she could towards the voice. There stood Olga, transfixed, pointing at the two bacon joints. Her eyes were full of tears. She said something in Romanian and turned away. It is hard to describe how I felt. I was almost in tears myself as I murmured to Addy, "I'm sorry! It was too soon. I should never have brought her here." Addy gently replied, "She has to see it sometime. She will be fine." The moment passed, Olga recovered and, as we walked home I mentally vowed that there was no way I would ever take her into the huge Sainsbury's store in the centre of Milton Keynes. (She was taken there, some weeks later, but not by me.) I was very conscious of the fact that she had to return home within a few weeks to the supermarkets in Romania where there is nothing worth buying. As we ate our meal that evening, we talked about our shopping expedition. Apparently what had upset Olga was seeing two joints of meat - and no queue! They were just sitting there and no one was buying them!

It reminded me of a story I had been told by someone else who had a visitor from one of the Eastern Bloc countries. They had passed the greengrocery department in a supermarket and the visitor exclaimed, "Oh, look! Bananas!" Her hostess, knowing that she had bananas at home, walked past, only to be brought back. "There are bananas. Aren't you going to buy them?" "No," she replied, "I don't need any." "But," persisted her guest, "they are **there**!" It is so difficult for us in the West to understand that, in Romania, if it's there you buy it, because it might not be there tomorrow.

The trip to the shops to purchase the shoes went quite smoothly. Many of the shoes Adriana liked were not suitable because of the current fashion for narrow heels. However we eventually found two pairs which she liked and bought both so that Bob would be able to advise us which would be preferable.

The rest of the week was filled up with visiting. Adriana was made very welcome by staff and pupils at White Spire School. We visited the hostel for the mentally handicapped next door to the church. Olga was very impressed with the facilities there and wondered if Nicoleta, her mentally handicapped daughter, would be able to come. We had to tell her it was not possible. We also had a conducted tour around the new private nursing home across the road. Everyone was so kind and welcoming.

Olga and Addy were clearly enjoying everything and revelling in what they were doing and seeing. Adriana, on the other hand, was very uncommunicative. There was no way to get inside the wall she had erected around herself. Occasionally we got a glimpse of the fun-loving girl underneath but then the shutters came down again. She would much rather watch TV than go out. It was an uphill struggle and language was a big problem. Adriana was obviously arguing with her mum much of the time (show me a teenager who doesn't) and Addy was trying to mediate. All this went on in Romanian, usually at the meal-table. We had discovered that Adriana actually understood the sense of most of what was said to her, but she resolutely refused to attempt to speak any English and disappeared to watch the TV as soon as she had finished her meal.

The situation eventually came to the boil and erupted in a violent temper tantrum at the weekend, followed by a very long sulk! It was a difficult situation all round. Olga was trying hard to pretend nothing was the matter as she was obviously embarrassed by Adriana's behaviour. Addy suddenly became very selective as to which bits of the conversation she translated for us, for obvious reasons. She did not feel she ought to translate family rows. I had to take her to one side and tell her it was important for us to know what was going on, however unpleasant it might be. Having brought two children of our own through the troublesome teens, I could make an educated guess at some of the problems but we could not hope to defuse a situation if we didn't know what was causing it.

Relationships were obviously becoming very strained and I felt so sorry for all of them. A normal teenager, after a row with Mum, would probably slam out of the room and fly upstairs to the comfort and security of her own room or go out for a walk. Adriana had no such outlet. She was still very much a prisoner - so she sulked. We decided the best policy was to try to ignore it and carry on as though nothing untoward was happening.

Soon it was time to go back to Ringwood for the fitting. This time we could do the journey there and back in a day. Bob examined the two pairs of shoes and decided on the most suitable. He pointed out to us that, if

Adriana had a second pair of shoes, the heel height must be absolutely identical to the first pair, otherwise there would be a danger of overbalancing. There was a slight discrepancy between the heels of the two pairs we had bought - although we thought they were identical. The good news was that Adriana's legs would be ready for collection in three days time. We would have to travel down and stay overnight again but once more George had all that under control.

Eventually the **big** day arrived. Adriana, Addy and Bob disappeared down the corridor and Olga and I waited for what seemed like an eternity. At last we were called into the room. There was Adriana, standing between the parallel bars. She was very tense. We watched as she hesitantly and painfully, walked the full length of the bars, coaxed along by Bob. At the end she collapsed on to a chair. The beads of perspiration ran down her face with the effort. It was a very emotional moment. When she'd walked back the length of the bars, Bob brought up the wheelchair for her to transfer into. What happened I am not quite sure but it seemed that she twisted herself, possibly forgetting that, wearing legs, it was not so easy to swing her body around. Whatever it was, it sparked off another sulk, which culminated in Adriana wheeling herself furiously into the ladies' room, where she whipped off her legs and threw them to one side. We were left in no doubt that there was to be no further co-operation that day!

As we left the hospital, with the legs in two very large brown paper bags in the boot of the car, Bob told us it was important for Adriana to wear the legs every day. "Start with one hour and work up until she is wearing them most of the time," he told us. That was going to be easier said than done, as we were soon to discover.

14: Problems arise

Although it was less than a month since our friends had arrived in England, it had been decided that, once the physio sessions began, Adriana and Olga would move to Anne and Ken's home. They lived very near to the clinic where the treatment was to take place and they also had a downstairs bedroom. Adriana would be unable to climb stairs when wearing her legs, always supposing she could be persuaded to wear them in the first place, so bags were packed and Olga and Adriana moved in with Anne and Ken. Addy moved in next door with their neighbour whose daughter, Tessa, was also an amputee and proved to be a great help and encouragement in the days ahead.

It was not easy for the Romanians, having to move on every few weeks but there was no other way we could cope for such a long period. All three had to start again in a different home with different ways of doing things. When Anne left for work in the morning she always left something in the 'fridge for their lunch - but on several memorable occasions came home to discover that what had been planned for dinner had, in fact, been eaten at lunchtime! Ken found it hard to acclimatise to Olga's late night hymn-singing before she went to bed!

We were all concerned about the fact that no one seemed able to break through the defensive wall Adriana had built around herself. Although she had lived with Roy and me for three weeks, we felt we knew her no better now than when we first met. Anne and Ken now came up against the same thing. We tried to think this through to discover what lay behind it and I also chatted it through with Geoff and a Christian psychologist. We came to the conclusion that Adriana was facing a host of problems which she did not even recognise. We kept reminding ourselves that she was a normal 16-year-old, with all the normal ups and downs of the teenage years. Added to that she had the trauma of a terrible accident and the consequent loss of body image, so important at that age. She had suffered a form of bereavement and had to go through the grieving process. She also probably felt rejected by those she thought were her friends who had not visited either in hospital or since she returned home. She had not just stood still psychologically and emotionally during the six months since the accident but had actually deteriorated.

Many of the difficulties we had encountered were only symptoms of the many problems, recognised and unrecognised, that Adriana had. Now she had different problems added, in that she was in a strange environment and was being thrown in at the deep end. From hiding away in her apartment, where she would not even sit on the balcony in case the neighbours saw her without legs, she was now being taken out almost every day and having to meet new people. She had probably dreamed about her new legs and, once they were fitted, the bubble burst as she realised some of the problems ahead. She was also probably very afraid. I tried to talk to her, through Addy, on one occasion. I explained that it was going to be hard work; that we would have to ask her to do many things she would rather not do; that she would probably get angry with anyone and everyone - especially me! She listened intently and said she understood but didn't think it would happen!

With all this in the background, we started the physiotherapy. Three one-hour sessions a week were scheduled. The legs were not being worn except at these sessions and so it took some time to put them on, but no time at all to whip them off when it was over! Olga obviously wanted to be there to see what was happening but it was equally obvious that Adriana concentrated harder when her Mum was not there to encourage or nag her! So I had to promote myself to Big Boss. Because they were in Anne's home, Anne was boss over certain things. However, as I had to liaise with all the medical authorities, make arrangements and arrange payments etc, we decided that it was necessary to have one supremo who had the final say - or we'd be here for a year and a day! So we made it clear who was in charge, making a joke out of it. "Anne, Sheila and Grace are all bosses - but I'm the **Big Boss**." In that position I was able to tell Olga she would not be going to any more physiotherapy sessions. She wasn't too happy but we gave her no choice.

Adriana could not be persuaded to wear her legs except for a few minutes each day and for her physio sessions. She still needed help in putting them on. By now she should have been wearing them for two to three hours a day and putting them on by herself. The physiotherapist was anxious to get her out of the parallel bars and on to sticks - but she had no confidence and clung on to the bars for support as she was afraid of falling. Not a lot of progress was being made.

One day, when sorting through a pile of papers and leaflets which had accumulated, I found a booklet entitled *Better Health for the Amputee* by H.E.S. Pearson, which had been sent to me by BLESMA some months earlier, before Adriana had even arrived in this country. One chapter suddenly began to make a great deal of sense. This would not have had much impact before but, as I shared it with the committee, we realised that, once again, the timing was just right. What we learned then was so helpful to us in understanding Adriana's situation.

The book explained how, losing a limb as the result of an accident affects every element of the patient's life in some way.

- the 'body-image' or sense of wholeness, which we normally take for granted is suddenly diminished by as much as one-sixth of its mass. (In Adriana's case it was more like one quarter.)

- the inability to carry out familiar tasks may be heightened by the presence of a 'phantom limb'. Adriana had told me she could still feel her legs and one was permanently curled up beneath her in the position it had been in when the train went over it.

- there can be the feeling that one has become conspicuous and an object of pity. This was certainly true and had been even more true at home in Romania.

- younger women who have lost a limb through accident or malignant disease have to face the same, and in some aspects more profound, psychological challenges as those of their male counterparts. Much of the amputee's future health depends on the success with which this heavy psychological burden can be accepted and dealt with by each individual. Adriana's whole future depended on how she learned to cope while she was here. There would be no back-up once she went back to Romania.

The article went on to describe how it was possible to make a rough division of the types of reaction to amputation into three groups. In the first are those with an exaggerated determination to overcome their disability. In the second are those with a defeatist and resigned attitude, with a strong tendency to depression, while the third group consisted of those with well-balanced personalities who manage to steer a course between those two extremes. There it was, in a nutshell!

Those in Group One can be a source of anxiety to those around them as their determination to dominate their environment could lead them into situations where their disability causes danger to themselves or others. Those in Group Three can take their normal place in society with the minimum of concessions.

There was no doubt in our minds that Adriana was at that moment in Group Two. The book went on to say that people in this group often had a constrictive and withdrawn attitude; needed a good deal of support and encouragement; lived lives that could be dominated by mourning for their lost capacity and by the fear of falling; tended to find fault with the limbfitters, doctors and relatives; have feelings of isolation, rejection and general inadequacy which may lead them to avoid human contact and normal social activities. It all fitted. It wouldn't have made sense to us before but it certainly did now. The $64,000 question now was, 'could Adriana ever move from this stage to take her full place in society?'

15: All change

Addy had now been here for more than four weeks, having initially only agreed to come for three. She was prepared to stay here over Christmas if necessary but we felt that was not fair to her or her husband, Paul-Dan. They had been married only eight months and it would be the only Christmas they would have together before their baby was born. It was important that she should be back in Romania for Christmas, as Paul-Dan would be home from the seminary for a few weeks.

Then we had a telephone call from some people in Edinburgh. Addy had acted as interpreter for them when they visited her church in Sibiu, around the time of her wedding. They would dearly love her to go and visit them for a few days! A simple request maybe, but it threw a spanner in the works here! We needed an interpreter for the physio sessions at the very least. Addy wanted to go to Edinburgh and we were reluctant to have to refuse. She had seen precious little of England during her stay, apart from Milton Keynes and the main roads between Bletchley and Ringwood! Ken had taken all three to London for a day but their activities had necessarily been very limited because of the wheelchair and other practical problems. We weren't sure how we would be able to manage without Addy but, on the other hand, she was doing a very demanding job and needed a few days' break. A friend, Rod Wallis, a lecturer at Milton Keynes College, had introduced us to another Romanian girl in her mid-twenties named Lavinia. She was living about 40 miles away in Desborough, but said she would come to help out and allow Addy to have these few days away. The tickets were booked, arrangements were made, Addy was put on the train to Edinburgh and Lavinia moved in. She was a delightful, vivacious girl, who spoke very good English and got on well with both Adriana and Olga. With the approach of Christmas came all the usual invitations to activities and special events, so Lavinia accompanied us.

We went to a concert by the Thames Valley Police Silver Band at the local Parish Church. It was a very enjoyable evening but we hadn't realised what an impression it had made on Adriana until we collected Addy from the station after her Edinburgh trip. I couldn't understand the full conversation going on in the car, but understood enough to pick out 'the police', 'music' and 'in the church'. Addy's voice echoed this incredulously "the **police**? **music**? in the **church**?" Of course - it was a concept that was quite foreign to them that the police should be invited to the church to give a concert.

A *Christmas Unwrapped* Cabaret Evening at our church and a Carol Service at the White Spire School also took place that week. Contacts made at both of these occasions were to lead to significant events in Adriana's rehabilitation, although none of us realised it at the time.

By now we had been told another interpreter had been found who was willing to come from Cluj before Christmas. However, when we checked Addy's ticket we found that the return date on it was 15th February 1991! We checked the other two tickets and discovered they all had the same date for return. This was despite the fact that Addy was supposed to be coming for three weeks, Olga was supposed to be going home before Christmas and Adriana had a six-month visa! We came to the conclusion that the clerk in the ticket office had either a birthday or a special anniversary on that day! When I tried to change the ticket I got the usual official Romanian response, "It is not possible!" There was nothing for it but to buy another ticket for the 'plane leaving Heathrow on Tuesday 18th December. Our new interpreter, Mihaela, would arrive that same evening. Rod Wallis, who had introduced Lavinia to us, offered to take Addy to Heathrow yo meet Mihaela. If Lavinia went too she would be able to fill Mihaela in on what was happening here.

We did not know that the date chosen for Addy's return journey and Mihaela's journey here was the date also chosen by the pilots and cabin crews of the Romanian airline, TAROM, to be the last before they went on indefinite strike over the Christmas period! However, once again the situation was smoothed out in a way which no one could have imagined or manufactured.

The plan was that Rod and Lavinia would say goodbye to Addy when the plane landed and rush round to the Arrivals to say hello to Mihaela. What is it they say about the best-laid plans? They arrived safely at Heathrow and waited - and waited. Because of the disruptions and strikes within TAROM, many of the planes were not where they were supposed to be in order to keep to their timetable. It now appeared that the incoming flight was so delayed that there was no slot for it to land in. It would be diverted to Luton and the passengers would be transferred to Heathrow by coach. Luton is much nearer to Milton Keynes and it seemed ridiculous to wait until Mihaela arrived at Heathrow - that could take hours. Addy assured them she would be fine and Rod managed to get a message through to Luton Airport for Mihaela, telling her to stay where she was until they could collect her. Rod found a group from Derbyshire who were travelling to Bucharest and asked them if they would keep an eye on Addy and make sure she did the right things at the right time and didn't arrive in Timbuctoo by mistake! He knew she was actually rather nervous of travelling alone. They were very happy to look after her, so Rod and Lavinia said farewell and set off for Luton.

John, one of the men in the group, asked Addy if she would keep an eye on their luggage while they went to collect some refreshment. She agreed to do this, and, as she waited for them to come back, noticed that the boxes they had with them were marked 'Bibles' and had RomAF labels on them! As soon as they returned, Addy asked John, "Are you a Christian? I see you are carrying Bibles." Of course he was! Addy was delighted. One problem was solved, but, unknown to them, another was looming.

Because the flight had landed at Luton, the pilot and cabin crew had decided that they did not have time to get back to Bucharest before the deadline for the strike to begin. As they could hardly go on strike when they were airborne, now seemed as good a time as ever. They would not be flying! What was to be done with all these passengers? They would be put up in a London hotel overnight while another flight was found for the morning. It happened that John knew of a church near the hotel where a midweek meeting was taking place, so, after they had found their rooms and eaten, they went to the meeting and spent a very happy time there.

We were at our housegroup Christmas party when I was called to the telephone to be told that Addy was still in London. Unfortunately she did not have enough change to complete the call or give her number before being cut off. All I knew was that she was still in England! It was weeks later when we heard the full story.

After their night in an hotel, they were told they would be flying with another airline to Budapest in Hungary, from where they would travel by train to Bucharest, a very long and tiring journey. Addy was not a good traveller at the best of times and being pregnant did not help. Her companion, John, had a very tight schedule already and was not sure how he could manage it if he lost a whole day. He was due to go to Dej, which is a town north of Addy's home town of Sibiu. She knew the way - he didn't. She knew the language - he didn't. They joined forces. She helped him to hire a car and he drove, while she acted as guide and interpreter! The others in his group went by rail. They managed to get a message to Addy's father, who then contacted her husband, Paul-Dan, to tell him not to wait at Bucharest airport but to meet Addy at their home in Sibiu.

By the time John and Addy reached the Romanian border it was almost 10pm. It had been a slow and tiring journey and it was obvious they would have to find somewhere to stay that night, and finish their journey the following day. As they drove through the town of Oradea, looking for somewhere to stay, Addy noticed a light in the window of a building. The building looked familiar. She had only been there once before but she recognised it as the Oradea Second Baptist Church. They stopped and knocked. The Church Administrator just happened to be there doing some work in the office! He immediately took control. Their car was driven into the church compound for overnight safety. Addy and John were whisked away by taxi to a church member's house, where they could have a very welcome rest. On the following day they set out on the last lap of the journey through heavy snow and eventually reached Cluj. There, John left Addy to take the short journey home to Sibiu by train while he went on to Dej. Who would ever think of writing such an unlikely ending to a story?

Mihaela eventually arrived and her story was also remarkable. She was only 20 and also on her first trip out of Romania. She had agreed to come for a month or two as she had no job. She was studying English in the hope of going on to further studies in the USA. Her parents were naturally anxious about her. After all, they knew nothing about us. Once again the RomAF contacts had been fruitful and we had found Mihaela by writing to a Romanian friend of Valerie. She told us that Mihaela was very shy, probably too shy and would have to be told exactly what to do.

During the ten days or so before Mihaela came, a number of students from Spurgeon's Baptist Theological College in London had been conducting a mission in various towns in Romania. They had been to Mihaela's church in Cluj. She told them she was coming to England - at that time the exact date was undecided - and her parents asked some of the students to try to make sure she was in good hands and keep an eye on her if they could. This, they promised to do.

When Mihaela turned up at Bucharest Airport on December 18th, the students just happened to be there waiting for the same plane, their mission ended. It also just happened that, because of all the delays to the planes and the uncertainty over the strikes, this was going to be the last plane out of Bucharest for some time. Again, the Lord's timing was impeccable. Mihaela was delighted to see some familiar faces. The students, on their part, were pleased to be able to help a pretty damsel in distress! They waited for four hours for the plane, while Mihaela got colder and colder, as the temperature was well below freezing. Eventually the students wrapped her in their sleeping bags as they sat in the unheated departure lounge. They looked after her until the plane touched down at Luton and she was met by Rod and Lavinia.

16: Breakthrough

Progress with Adriana's rehabilitation continued to be slow. The legs still went to physiotherapy in brown paper bags, accompanied by Adriana in the wheelchair. There was some improvement - she had left the security of the parallel bars and launched out with two sticks - but it was slow progress. It wasn't that Adriana did not co-operate. She did everything she was told to do and worked very hard while she was in the gym but was just not doing enough in between. She could walk up and down in the gym but was still too dependent on the wheelchair at home. There were also tensions between Adriana and her mother which were surfacing more often but it was difficult to get to the bottom of them.

On one occasion we were all talking together and I happened to ask whether Adriana would be able to return to her school once she was back in Romania. Apparently that would be out of the question as it necessitated catching two trolley-buses each way. That would clearly be impossible. A lively conversation ensued in Romanian between Olga and Adriana which erupted into a full-scale temper tantrum. I turned to Lavinia for interpretation. She said, "There are problems. Olga says she has been told there is a very good school for the handicapped in Iaşi. Adriana says she will not go there" - the understatement of the year! For once I was on Adriana's side. What was the point of all this hard work to rehabilitate her if she was to end up in a school for the handicapped? It took time for this to be explained to Olga but at last she seemed to understand. It didn't solve the problem of which school Adriana would go to but it cleared the air.

It also became obvious that Olga was not pleased about being excluded from the physiotherapy sessions. It had been necessary and had resulted in improvement but, as a mother, she was anxious to see what was happening to her daughter. We knew Adriana did not want her there, so that made it difficult. It was time for the Big Boss to take control. Knowing how difficult 16-year-olds can be, I nevertheless told Olga that I would take her to the physiotherapy session myself on December 27th - a day they would be spending with us. Adriana need not be told until it happened. Olga was satisfied and that eased the situation for a while.

When Mihaela arrived we briefed her on what was expected. It was important for her to realise that we needed to know what was going on between mother and daughter so we could take steps to defuse some of the more volatile situations. Her English was not as good as Addy's or

Lavinia's and she was really very young and immature to come into that situation. Under the circumstances she coped pretty well. She was much nearer Adriana's age and they got on well together. She told me that she had the impression from Adriana that there was no hurry to learn to walk. After all, when we had been asked how long she would be here for, we had said "As long as it takes!" We had said that because we had had no idea at that stage how long it **would** take. Adriana seemed to have understood that she could take her time! That put the cat among the pigeons in our committee! A push was needed so it was time for another Big Boss act. Adriana was told that, as the return date on her ticket was February 15th, then that was the date she would be going back. She would have to pull her socks up (metaphorically speaking, of course)!

We had also decided that, once Christmas was over, Olga must go home to her family. She had made up her mind before she came that she was staying until after Christmas. That was fair enough, but I told her through Mihaela, that she must go home in January. It was necessary for the family to be prepared. They needed to know what was happening and what to expect when Adriana returned home. There might be some bathroom aids that would need to be fixed. If so, she could take them and make sure they were installed before Adriana arrived home. Olga understood and accepted what was said.

We began to realise that one of the reasons why Adriana removed her legs after physio was because she did not think she would be able to get into the car while she was wearing them. Without legs it was very easy to swing from the wheelchair into the front passenger seat. One evening Ann, the physio, decided to show her. We wheeled her outside and then she walked the few paces to the car. Unfortunately there was a slight slope instead of a kerb. Adriana's worst fear was realised - she fell down! As we picked her up and dusted her down, the physiotherapist said matter-of-factly, "OK, so now you've had your fall and you know it's nothing to worry about. You'll have more before you're finished." Getting into the car was not as difficult as she had feared; yet another hurdle overcome.

Anne's neighbour, Tessa, came round once or twice to encourage Adriana and help her to overcome various problems with her legs. Adriana was beginning to find it easier to put them on and would wear them a little longer but it was nowhere near enough to make the kind of progress needed and she would still not wear them when she was going out. Bob had said to me at one of the fittings, "Unfortunately, we are going to have to ask Adriana to grow up very, very quickly". It was not an easy transition for her.

Two days before Christmas it was necessary to move Adriana and Olga again, this time to Sheila and Peter's home, with Mihaela just around the corner in another home. The weeks were flying by. Christmas came and went and our three Romanian guests really saw what an English Christmas was like. Each day of the holiday they spent with a different family. It could have caused problems if people had gone overboard as far as Christmas presents were concerned but once again the church folk took to heart what had been suggested and gave small, useful gifts; things that could be packed easily or eaten before leaving England! Romanian culture is very different to ours and one of the things many people found difficult to grasp was our guests' apparent lack of interest in or appreciation of the gifts they were given. These would often just be put to one side, still wrapped, to be opened later in private, so one never knew if they were appreciated. It was only much later, when we took Adriana home to Romania, that we realised fully just how much every gift was valued.

At the end of Christmas Day I went to bed with my mind full of questions about what we could do to speed up the rehabilitation process. There was a limit to how long we could all keep up this pace and we desperately needed a breakthrough. There were signs of progress, but not enough. In the early hours of the morning I woke suddenly. It was almost as though a voice had actually spoken to me. "What Adriana needs now is two week's intensive walking training on a residential basis." That was all: no further clues.

When I woke again - at a more reasonable hour - that thought was still there. Had it just been a dream? Was it the next logical step? If so, where on earth did one start? I needed some professional advice. On December 27th we entertained the Romanians for the day and I took Adriana to her physio session. Olga came too, as we'd promised. She was happy to see what was going on and the progress that had been made and I was pleased to see that she kept well in the background and just watched. Afterwards I had a quick word with Ann the physio about the thought that had come to me in the night. "Perfect! It's just what she needs," was her comment. She didn't know where we would be able to go on a private basis but certainly thought we ought to make enquiries about the possibilities. She didn't tell me until much later that she had recently gone home after one of the physio sessions and told her husband, "I don't know how to tell those church people that they are wasting their money. That girl will never walk."

There was no doubt that now was the time for a big push if we were to see any results. We were really reaching for the moon and there were times when we wondered if we were asking too much of Adriana. She would manage to walk eventually, if we gave her time, but time was something we did not have in abundance. However, underlying everything was this deep peace. We **knew** God was in control as we had seen His hand at work in so many fine details. He had led us into this and He would lead us and Adriana through the difficulties.

After the physio session on December 27th we had a visit from Paul Wedrychowski and his girl friend, Maxine. They now had all the proceeds of the sponsored run which Paul had organised at the Castlethorpe Keep-Fit Club in September. It had taken place on the only wet Saturday of the summer, when the weather was absolutely atrocious. Paul and Maxine wanted to hand over the cheque and meet Adriana at the same time. They had raised the amazing sum of just over £1,100! Castlethorpe is only a small village and I think every single person there had been cajoled into taking some part, either running, sponsoring or offering prizes!

The old year passed and 1991 began. 1990 had been a pretty momentous year for our church and also for our Romanian friends. What did the New Year have in store? At around midnight on 2nd January, just as we were settling down to sleep, the telephone rang. It was Dave Griffin. Apologising for the lateness of the call, he said "You remember my sister who met Adriana at the Cabaret Evening? Well, she has had experience of another amputee, an elderly lady, who had also rejected her artificial legs. She has made a suggestion I think you ought to hear." That woke me up! Anything would help. Dave went on, "Adriana is obviously embarrassed at her legs being seen. Why don't you buy her a pair of jeans? They would cover her legs and make her look more like a normal teenager." What a simple and yet brilliant idea! If she wore jeans she would not be able to whip the legs off quite so easily, as she would need to remove the jeans first. That would be difficult in company! It was the perfect solution. Although we had always intended to purchase such items before Adriana returned to Romania it had not entered our heads to do it yet. We were too busy sorting out the nitty-gritty of their timetable and physiotherapy sessions. However, it was clearly time to re-think our priorities.

It was obvious the more we thought about it. The new legs which Adriana now had, although very natural looking to us, were not **her** legs. They did not even look like **her** legs. To a young girl of sixteen, that was very important. If someone loses one limb, there is the probability that the limbfitter can match the artificial one to the remaining limb. When both limbs have gone there is nothing to go by. No legs, however well made, however natural they looked to outsiders, could ever be the same for Adriana as the ones she had lost. While she had been taking them to the physio sessions in their brown paper bags in the car boot, and only putting them on in the gym, a skirt had been essential. Now she put them on at home, it made no difference what she wore.

It was no sooner suggested than done! Two days later two of our young people took Adriana and Mihaela into Central Milton Keynes on a shopping expedition and bought Adriana a pair of jeans and a shirt. She was delighted with the jeans. She wore them all day. It was working. She could not take the legs off without first going upstairs to her room. Going upstairs was still very difficult and she only did it once a day - at bedtime. It was a case of 'go to bed early so the legs can come off' or 'watch the rest of the film and just stick it out'. The film won and a very uncomfortable Adriana had worn her legs for a whole day. It wasn't long before we began to wonder if we could get the jeans off her for long enough to wash them!

Grace was very worried about the fact that Adriana was obviously not doing enough of the exercises to make a significant improvement in her walking. One of the problems was that Sheila and Peter both left home for work early in the morning and therefore there was no supervision. Although Olga was up early, Adriana didn't emerge from her bedroom until well over half the morning had passed, therefore Mihaela didn't arrive until she knew Adriana would be up and about. The exercises were being done in the privacy of her bedroom, after a fashion, but not enough, and the whole structured day we had tried to establish was in danger of collapse. It was time something was done to stop the slide. Grace had a week's leave due to her and offered to travel over to Sheila's home first thing every morning to do half an hour's exercises with Adriana - an offer we gratefully accepted. We gave Adriana no choice in the matter. Within days there was a marked improvement, although the sessions were not always very popular, particularly as they took place so early in the morning (before 9am). Sheila and Peter continued the impetus by encouraging Adriana to venture out into the small park by their home when they took the dog for a walk.

Our committee now decided that Adriana's reliance on the wheelchairs had to be broken. She still had one upstairs for bedroom/bathroom use and one downstairs. One must go. So Anne turned up one evening and gaily announced that the Red Cross needed their wheelchair back so she had come to take it away! There was no arguing with that - and off it went in the boot of her car. Adriana was beginning to learn to stand on her own two feet in more ways than one. Things were beginning to look more hopeful.

17: Ups and downs

It soon became obvious that there were difficulties in the relationship between Olga and Mihaela, and on several occasions we had to do a bit of trouble-shooting. The basic problem seemed to be that Olga expected more from Mihaela than she was prepared to give. Having brought up a family of nine children, most of whom were now older than Mihaela, Olga treated her as she would one of her own and expected her to toe the line. If she didn't agree with what Mihaela did, she said so! Mihaela, on the other hand, came from a very small family and a totally different background. Although I could talk things through with Mihaela I could only talk to Olga **through** Mihaela. Therein lay a problem because it became obvious we were only getting one side of any story. Mihaela was also unwell and extremely homesick, as it was her first time away from home and she had been plunged into a very complex situation among a lot of strangers. It just was not going to work.

Sheila, Anne, Grace and I discussed this and, as always, came to a unanimous decision. We had each come to realise that, although Adriana was still not speaking English, there was little that she did not understand. One particular incident, on Boxing Day, stood out clearly as an example. Adriana, Olga and Addy were being entertained by Grace and her husband, Stuart, for the day. During a meal, Stuart made some cheeky, teasing remark to Grace which was meant for her ears alone. Adriana, sitting next to Grace, almost fell off her chair laughing. Humour, in a foreign language, is not easily understood but there was no doubt that Adriana understood it perfectly. It clearly demonstrated the extent of her understanding of the English language. It was becoming apparent that the need for an interpreter was not as great as it had been at the beginning. If the need became desperate we might be able to call on Lavinia's services again. It was time to think about arranging homeward flights, not only for Olga but also for Mihaela.

At that time there was a great deal of international tension after the invasion of Kuwait by Iraq. There was a possibility of war. Although Romania would not be directly involved in any possible conflict, if it happened we did not know how it would affect the oil situation and Romania imports almost all of her crude oil from Iraq. It also put a large question mark over international flights - as if there weren't enough question marks over the TAROM flights already.

We could not do anything immediately so Grace, Adriana, Mihaela and

I set off to visit Stoke Mandeville Hospital to find out what kind of aids Adriana needed for complete independence in the bathroom. Once we had that worked out, Olga could go home to prepare the family and tell Peter about any necessary adjustments that should be made to the apartment. I had measurements and a plan of the bathroom back home in Ploieşti so that we could see what would and would not be useful. Eventually, after much discussion with the occupational therapist at the hospital, we found that Adriana would be able to manage perfectly with a bathboard across the bath and a bath seat inside. No fixing to walls needed - only the simplest of aids were necessary. We went home well satisfied and placed the necessary order. Complete independence was well within sight.

Meantime I was still pursuing this 'dream' of residential, intensive walking training. We needed someone in a white coat to come in to Adriana each morning and say "Time for exercise" and again each afternoon. We felt that, if we really were being guided on to the next step, then there would be a place somewhere where this would be done. All we had to do was find it. So I started where I had started originally - with the organisations for the disabled. I rang Mr Sladen at The Limbless Association and outlined what we felt was necessary. "Am I asking the impossible?" I asked. "Is there any such place?" His reply was reassuring. "Yes, I'm sure we could find somewhere," he said, promising to do some research and come back to me. It didn't take him long to come up with a number for me to contact in Oxford.

It took about three weeks to make all the arrangements and get all the details sorted out. During that time life became very difficult. We could not tell Adriana because she would worry and probably refuse to go. It had to come as a *fait accompli*. Because Mihaela and Adriana were so close, we could not risk telling Mihaela, in case it slipped out in conversation. There was no way we could tell Olga, who really ought to have known what was going on, because we could only do it through Mihaela. The situation was becoming very complicated.

Olga was obviously unhappy and it was becoming increasingly difficult to communicate with her because of the tension. The committee had an emergency meeting to discuss and pray over the situation together. There was no alternative - we would have to split the three of them up in some way. Eventually it was agreed that Mihaela should move in with Adriana and that Olga should come to our home. The official reason for this was to see how Adriana coped without her Mum around - it would be a trial separation before Olga left for Romania, which, although they did not know it yet, was less than two weeks away.

Just to add to the complications, one of the students who had helped

Mihaela on her journey to England rang her to ask if she could go to London - on January 19th! I just had to tell Mihaela it wasn't possible, without giving an adequate reason, as we were still in the middle of negotiations over the two-week course and trying to book the flights for sometime that weekend. All I could say was that we were negotiating the next step in Adriana's rehabilitation and that weekend was not possible. In any case, on a cultural basis, it was a tricky situation. In the Romanian churches a young, single girl would not be allowed to spend a day in a strange city with a young man she hardly knew, even if he was a fellow Christian. Although Mihaela was living in our country and our culture, she was returning to her parents and pastor, who would be expecting us to look after her in what they considered was a Christian way. I didn't rate very high in the popularity stakes at that particular time, but it couldn't be helped. The rehabilitation was the most important thing, not being flavour of the month! The situation was resolved when Mihaela was invited to a party in a church member's home before she left, and the student was invited too.

Next time Dave drove us down to Ringwood, we left Olga in Bletchley and Sheila took her out for the day. It was certainly easier travelling with only four in the car. It was only a quick visit, so, as it was a beautiful day Dave made a detour on the way home and took us to Mudeford, a small village on the Dorset coast, where we spent a little time walking along the promenade.

On the way home, Mihaela said to me, "Margaret, I would really like to have an English Bible". As she comes from the University city of Cluj and, as Bibles had been pouring in since the revolution, I was surprised she didn't already have one. It turned out that she did have an English Bible but it was the King James version. She wanted a modern translation which was easier to read. "That's no problem," I replied, "we'll go over to the Christian bookshop one day and buy one for you." She looked a little puzzled. "How much do they cost?" she asked. "That all depends on what you want. Anything from £6 up to about £30, I suppose" was my answer. After a short pause, while she digested this information, she turned to me and said "But do you have to **buy** Bibles? In Romania we get them **free!**" She had no idea that they receive them free of charge because Christians here and in other countries give sacrificially to allow that to happen.

The move was arranged. Adriana and Mihaela would stay with Anne again and Olga would come to us. It wouldn't be easy having her here without an interpreter but we felt that she needed some space, time and tender loving care before going back home. She and I could communicate on a very basic level. The problem was that I needed to talk more deeply with her about Adriana's future life back in Romania but just couldn't do it through Mihaela. This time together could give us the opportunity, if only I had the language. Once more I shared the problem with Valerie at the RomAF office - and once more she had a possible solution. "What about Rodica?" she suggested. Rodica Bradbury is Romanian, married to an Englishman. An older lady, deeply spiritual, she would be able to minister to Olga in her own language, in a way I never could. There was no time to be lost. Although I had seen Rodica at the 1990 RomAF Annual Conference, I had never actually met her. I rang her at her home in Leicester and she agreed to come at very short notice. Events were falling into place once again.

On Sunday 13th January 1991, the morning of their move, the service had already started and Adriana was not there. That was most unusual - was she ill? Suddenly there was movement by the door. We turned to see Adriana **walking** into church for the first time, followed by Sheila, who had engineered it all and looked very pleased with herself! There was a spontaneous round of applause from the members of the congregation. It was a very moving moment and one we had all been waiting for. Another step in the right direction.

After church was over, the moves took place. There were times when they must have felt like pieces on a chessboard, but these moves were needed for everyone's sake. Now we were all in the right places for the next phase and I waited anxiously for Rodica's arrival the following day. Even that was to become significant as we discovered when we turned up at the coach station to meet her.

Because the coach was very late, our car was not available and we needed to take a taxi. Instead of 'phoning from the box, I popped into the waiting room where I had heard a man speaking to his office about taxis and fares. "Can you find us a taxi or do I have to telephone from over there?" I asked. It was his job to link coach and bus station with his minibus. As we were almost on his route, he said he would take us. We climbed aboard, Rodica and I sitting behind him, as she wanted to be filled in as quickly as possible about the situation and what we wanted from her. As we talked, the driver butted in once or twice on the totally different subject of the possible Gulf War and this being the possible end of the world civilisation as we know it. Rodica had the gift of the evangelist. Our conversation was forgotten as she warmed to her subject and explained to him what the Bible had to say. When we reached home, he drove onto the drive outside our front door and said "This is all very interesting. I could listen to you for a long time." "Do you have time?" we asked. "Oh, yes!" he replied, "they don't need me at work at the moment."

He refused an invitation to come into the house as he needed to be in radio contact with his base. Olga and I came indoors, put the kettle on, made a cup of tea and waited - and waited - and waited. By now Rodica had her Bible out and they were deep in conversation. They didn't want tea - she was introducing him to the God who offers 'living water'. Half an hour later, Rodica came in, beaming. "He has accepted the Lord," she told us. What a way to arrive!

Now all the arrangements for the next few weeks had been made, we had to tell our friends what was happening. I had managed to book flights for Olga and Mihaela on January 20th and we had fixed up the residential two weeks of walking training for Adriana, starting on January 28th. I briefed Rodica on the whole situation and, together, we talked it through with Olga. The only thing Olga was worried about was how Adriana would eventually return home but the committee had suggested the obvious solution would be for Grace and me to accompany her on the journey back to Ploieşti so that we could be there to see how she coped with those 39 steps and the bathroom and to help the family and the church come to terms with the new Adriana. It was such a relief to be able to tell Olga what was going on and she was equally relieved to be able to discuss things at length. Once again, the right person had been brought into our orbit at just the right time. At last I went to bed, leaving Olga and Rodica talking, sharing, reading the Scriptures together and praying together in Romanian. It was just what Olga needed at that moment. There was a certain amount of healing needed. We did not underestimate the emotional turmoil she had been going through. It was good to know that she trusted us so completely to do what was right for Adriana. She didn't question any of the decisions we had had to make without her. Rodica was certainly used to minister just what Olga needed during those few brief days.

The problem now arose of what to do with Adriana during the week after her Mum returned to Romania and before she went to Oxford. A full, structured programme for each day was essential - and, once again, we were all out at work. I telephoned Mr George Atherton, headmaster of White Spire School. We had a good link with the school as Roy went in to visit them every week. The staff and children had taken a great interest in Adriana and her progress. When they first heard about her they took a special collection at their morning Assembly. The pupils had had no notice of this collection and gave willingly of their pocket money, which we found very touching. Would it be possible for them to have her in their midst for a week? There was no way she would be able to cope with the rough and tumble of a normal comprehensive school with the usual mad dash along the corridors between lessons. Although she was now walking short distances with two sticks, she was not confident among crowds. Would they allow us to take her there each morning and collect her when we came home from work? There was no problem, Mr Atherton assured me. They'd be delighted to have her. They would also give her a midday meal and if she became tired she could retire to the Senior Pupils' Common Room and watch the TV. We knew she would be safe and in good hands there and were very grateful.

Rodica stayed with us for three days. On the second day I brought Adriana and Mihaela to our home. It was time for them to know what was happening now that Rodica and I had discussed the plans with Olga and everything was clear. Mihaela and Olga would be flying home to Romania at the end of that week. Adriana would spend the following week at White Spire School after which she would go to Oxford for two weeks' intensive training then back to Dorset Orthopaedic for new sockets for her limbs. Then she would go home - probably around the end of February.

We felt it was important to speak to each of them separately. Mihaela was first. We explained that we realised how homesick she had been and that not being well had made things much more difficult for her. She herself had told us that Adriana understood enough English not to need an interpreter. With all that in mind, and with the possible imminence of war in the Gulf, we had booked her ticket home. She was not immediately sure how to react - but only for a split second, then she beamed delightedly. She was going home. She couldn't wait to tell Adriana! By the time it was Adriana's turn to find out what was happening, she already knew most of it. Her face was as black as thunder. We were not in for an easy ride with this one!

18: Left alone

Adriana listened in stony silence as I outlined the plan for the next stage in her rehabilitation. To say she was not happy was to put it mildly. It was obvious that, beneath the questioning, she was scared. Who wouldn't be? It was yet another new situation for her to cope with. How would she manage once her Mum and Mihaela had left? Would there ever be an end to it? How many more things would she have to do? Why hadn't we just left her in peace at home?

She needed reassurance and encouragement. She was going to feel bereft when her mother left. Mums are good buffers on which to vent your wrath when you feel threatened. They had been together constantly since Adriana's accident and we knew neither of them would find it easy to part. On the other hand, they both needed a bit of space and we were certain this was the right way forward. I promised Adriana that she would not be left with strangers while she was in Oxford. We would make sure somehow that there was always someone she knew with her. It was very much a one-way conversation! She needed time to take it in. We had discovered before that, if given time to think things through, Adriana usually accepted them, but her initial reaction to anything new was always "No".

Later in the evening we took Mihaela and Adriana back to Anne's and Olga, Rodica and I had some time together. How much Olga and I appreciated those few days with Rodica. There was so much we needed to share and it just had not been possible until then. I knew Olga was going back to Romania with fresh hope for Adriana's future because we were beginning to see some signs of real progress being made.

A church family took Adriana out for the day and she returned sporting a new pair of training shoes to wear with her jeans. Everyone admired them. She looked great - just like any other teenager - and she obviously felt great too.

Angela, a teacher and a church member, offered to give Adriana English lessons. She was still not saying more than a few words, although she understood most of what was said to her. Direct questions were answered, usually with as few words as possible! "Yes" and "No" seemed to fit the bill a lot of the time. It boiled down once more to lack of confidence. If Mihaela was going home, Adriana was going to have to cope alone. We believed she could do it - but she didn't! Angela scoured the local teachers' centre for suitable books and the work began. Adriana co-operated as usual and did the homework she was set.

Before Olga and Mihaela left, there was some important shopping to be done. A new Bible was duly purchased for Mihaela and, one morning, Olga and I set out for Central Milton Keynes. She had been very frugal with what little money she had and the reason now became apparent. She wanted to buy some gifts for each member of her very large family. It took us all of six hours to make all the necessary purchases and when we eventually arrived home we collapsed in an exhausted heap! We had looked at many things but she found everything so expensive here. She wasn't looking for expensive fripperies or luxury items. It was illuminating to see the care with which she chose the items she eventually took home: tights, deodorants, soap for her daughters; socks, razors and blades for the men; pants for the grandchildren - everyday items here but either unobtainable or expensive luxuries back home in Romania.

There was no way Olga could pack everything she had accumulated during her time here and stay within her luggage allowance for the journey home. Many people had given her items of clothing for her family. There had also been many gifts given to Addy for her new baby when it arrived, which she had not been able to take with her. They all had to be packed into cardboard boxes, carefully labelled and put on a lorry which was going out to Romania with a load of aid from RomAF. They would reach their destination eventually, we hoped.

Once again we had had the same problem that we had with Addy over the date on their return tickets and ended up having to purchase singles. Then we learned that TAROM was on strike for an indefinite period, starting 12th January. That was all we needed! After a number of frantic telephone calls we discovered that they were not actually on strike but had internal organisational problems. However, we were assured they would be starting again on 20th January, so we booked the tickets for that date and hoped for the best!

One final thing was important before Olga left. She needed to know that Adriana could now be completely independent in the bathroom. The bathroom aids which we had ordered had arrived, so now was the time to try them out. There was no problem. She managed perfectly. We showed Olga how to adjust them to fit the bath at home and she was happy. She did not need to take anything back with her to screw into walls or fit around pipes. These simple aids were all that were needed and no longer would she need to strain to lift Adriana into and out of the bath. Adriana delighted in her new independence. She could have a long, leisurely bath, taking her own time, without any interference - and she lost no time in doing so! It was great!

Very soon the day arrived for Olga and Mihaela to leave us. We checked that the planes were definitely flying that day before setting off for Heathrow Airport. It was still a bit hit-and-miss as we had to collect the tickets from the travel agent at the airport. However, all went smoothly. There were hugs all round and then they disappeared beyond passport control and were on their way.

Now Adriana was alone. She moved back in with Roy and me, as we were nearest to White Spire School. The staff and pupils were all very kind to her at the school but she was always glad when it was home-time. It was tiring for her, but we were pleased that at last she was having a fully structured day. I took her in the morning by car, without the wheelchair, and left her to walk around the school during the day. When I went to collect her I walked to the school with the wheelchair but suggested she should walk as far as she could before collapsing into it! Each day she walked a little further. I could see that she was setting herself targets. "Just to the next lamp-post." "Just as far as that opening." It was encouraging. By the end of the week she was almost making it to our front door, a distance of several hundred yards from the school.

Now the legs were being worn constantly. Adriana was accepting them and even beginning to be able to laugh at them. At night they would be left sitting on the ottoman in her bedroom, complete with jeans and shoes, ready to slip on the next day. As I passed them, I would say, "Excuse me, please!" At first, I think she thought I was making fun of her disability but the day came when, in manoeuvring her wheelchair in the bedroom, one of the feet got in the way. "Excuse me, **please!**" said Adriana, laughing, as she headed for the door!

The time was drawing nearer for Adriana to go to Oxford and she was becoming very tense. She clammed up whenever it was mentioned. One evening I sat down with her and explained to her the many ways we had been led through this rehabilitation programme. I reminded her of what she'd been told very early on, that there would be times when she would feel very angry - with me in particular. That produced the vestige of a smile in her otherwise set face. I assured her that we loved her and that we were only doing what we believed was right for her long-term future; I spelt out many of the things that had happened, which we realised could only have happened because the Lord was in control; and I told her how amazed we had been at the way every little detail had come together at the right time. Because of the care He had taken over those smallest details, we were sure that the Lord had some very special plan for her life once she was back in Romania. She listened politely, but I could see she was not convinced.

19: Oxford

Working out a rota for people to stay over in Oxford wasn't easy but we had promised Adriana she would not be alone while she was there. Lavinia agreed to spend a couple of nights with her to begin with, as we felt it would be helpful to have someone she could communicate with in her own language at the start. It might help her to feel a little more at ease. Pat Boyd from East Sussex, who had been beavering away raising prayer support and persuading all her friends to give to our Adriana Fund also agreed to come up and stay for a few nights. A bed was made available in Adriana's room for the carer. Unfortunately, just a day or so before we were due to go, Lavinia was ill and unable to go, so I had to step in and take her place.

On Sunday 27th January 1991, I set off for Oxford with a very subdued Adriana. We were due to report to the hospital at 9am on the Monday morning. Our son, Andrew, shared a house with three others in Oxford and they made space for us overnight. That helped to take Adriana's mind off what was to come but all too soon Monday morning arrived. We were warmly welcomed at the hospital and shown to the room which would be her home for the next two weeks.

After we'd settled in, there were long gaps between visits from nurses, doctors, limbfitters etc. To fill in the time, after we had tired of playing the games we'd taken, I produced the photograph we had of all her family. "Who are these people?" I asked. She looked surprised. "My family," she replied. "I don't know anything about your family," I said. "Can you tell me who they all are and a little bit about each of them?" She looked at me as though I was slightly crazy, then realised that I was wanting her to speak English. With a wry smile and a resigned sigh, she began hesitantly at first, "This is my sister. Her name is Faby. She is married to Vasile and they have two children, Sergius and Emanuel." We went through all nine children and her parents, then her brothers-in-law and grandmother who weren't on the photograph. She did very well. Shortly afterwards, the consultant arrived to examine Adriana. He saw the photograph lying there and asked her about her family. She went through it all again with him, without faltering. He was most impressed and said "I thought you didn't speak much English!" She was delighted and it was easy to see that it had boosted her confidence.

With two one-hour sessions of physio each day, Adriana's walking improved rapidly. Grace reported back after her stay at the hospital,

"They had to take one of her legs away for re-alignment today - just for one hour. When they'd taken it Adriana said, 'At first, I didn't like to wear my legs. Now I don't like to take them off'."

When I reported this to Ann, the Milton Keynes physio, she flung her arms in the air and whooped with delight. "We've cracked it!" she exclaimed, "This is what I've been waiting to hear!" It was only then that she told me of her initial reservations and how she had told her husband that she did not believe Adriana would ever walk.

Other people too were making sure that Adriana had company during this time. Andrew and his whole housegroup visited her one evening instead of having their usual meeting. From what I heard, that was a very lively gathering. Knowing her love of bananas and oranges they filled her fruit bowl to overflowing! Members of staff from the *Baptist Times* office at Didcot also came along to visit her, including one girl who is herself an amputee. There was plenty to keep her busy and the two hours walking every day made her very tired. She soon began to realise that, far from being bored or afraid, she was actually enjoying herself! She also got on well with Mary, her physiotherapist. Now she had gained a little bit of confidence in conversation we were able to get through to the real Adriana and discovered a lively, fun-loving personality. The protective wall she had erected around herself was beginning to crumble and the real person was emerging at last.

Then came an unexpected blow. We had planned to take Adriana back to Ringwood after the two weeks at Oxford to have new sockets fitted, then take her home around the end of February, not too far from the ultimatum date we had given her of 15th February. However, the limbfitter at Oxford said he felt it would be better for her to remain here for a further five or six weeks of walking practice before her sockets were changed. It would obviously be several months before she would be able to walk unaided but, as she grew more confident and walked more, her stumps would shrink rapidly and the sockets would soon be too large once more. It made sense but meant we had to rethink our strategy.

Once again we came up against the problem of boredom and safety while we were at work, whichever home she stayed in. While at work, I talked it over with Valerie and, once again, we found a possible solution. "Have you thought of Thornton College?" she asked. Thought of it? I hadn't even **heard** of it! Where and what was Thornton College? It turned out to be a convent school which took boarders and it is situated about 12 miles from Bletchley, near Buckingham. They took boarders on a weekly as well as a termly basis because it was in a rural area and it was not always possible for girls to get in and out each day. It sounded good. What sounded even better was the fact that they had previously had a double amputee as a pupil, so they would have no problem coping with Adriana's disability. Furthermore, as they had a link with a Spanish school and often had girls from Spain who had very little English, they offered a course of English as a Foreign Language!

I could hardly believe it, although I should have been getting used to these things happening by now! Once again we had the perfect solution to our problem. Now all we had to do was to ask the Sisters at the College if they could take Adriana for the half-term up to the Easter holidays. I had little doubt what the answer would be, even before I asked. I telephoned Thornton College and explained the situation to the secretary. The Headmistress, Sister Brenda, would need to consult the members of staff concerned. We realised there would be fees to pay, but now we had no worries over that, as we had far exceeded our original target. We were completely free to go ahead with anything that would help Adriana's rehabilitation, without worrying that we might not be able to afford it. Within a few days they rang back and said they would like to help. Could I go over to Thornton and talk to the Headmistress about what was required? We made a date for the following week.

Adriana's first week at Oxford was soon over and it was time to come home. Unknown to her, plans had been made for the next day. If she was hoping to have a leisurely lie-in on that Saturday morning, she was doomed to disappointment.

Some weeks previously, down at St Leonard's Hospital at Ringwood, browsing through a leaflet about BASA (British Amputee Sports Association) I had noticed they had regular Sports Training Weekends at Stoke Mandeville Hospital. It sounded as though it was something which might help Adriana, to see other amputees taking part in various sports. It might just help her to realise that other people had similar disabilities and that meaningful life for her had not ended under the wheels of that train the previous April. I wrote and asked for details of future events and discovered that there would be one taking place on February 2nd - 4th and we would be welcome to take Adriana along for the day on the Saturday. What was more, they gave her free membership of BASA for one year.

We didn't tell her where we were going until she was ready to go out - by now we had discovered this was the best policy. It was just a case of "We'll be going out at 10 o'clock tomorrow morning. Make sure you're ready." She was always ready on time. We loaded up the wheelchair and Roy, Adriana, Grace and I set off for the Sports Centre at Stoke Mandeville.

By the time we arrived, Adriana had been told where we were going. We were greeted and shown around by Margaret Baker, wife of John Baker, the current Chairman of BASA. We all decided that we would view the outdoor sports first as it was the sort of morning where the chill strikes right into your bones. One of the girls demonstrated the shot putt and we watched as a young man was shown how to throw the javelin. He looked perfectly normal in his track suit - then we were informed that he had lost a leg three months earlier and had only been wearing his artificial leg for six weeks. That made Adriana sit up and take notice!

Once the chilly weather started to get to us we wheeled Adriana indoors and took the lift up to the viewing area above the main sports hall. We were all transfixed as we watched. It was a real eye-opener for Roy, Grace and myself and it was hard to imagine what Adriana must have felt. Young people, all amputees, most wearing their special sports legs, were playing volleyball and badminton. Others were taking part in wheelchair basketball. If we wanted to broaden her horizons we had certainly come to the right place.

After watching intently for half an hour or so we went back downstairs and wheeled her into the hall. Grace said cheerily, "How about a game of table-tennis, Adriana?" That suggestion was obviously considered a rather sick joke and she received a firm "No" for an answer. Undeterred by this response, she wheeled Adriana across to the table-tennis table and parked her there while she went off to find some bats and a ball. Soon she was hitting gentle balls across the table to a reluctant Adriana who hit them back if she could reach them and kept Roy and me very busy as ballboys! Soon she began to relax. After half an hour or so, we were getting hungry with all this unaccustomed exercise but Adriana was just beginning to enjoy herself. We managed to prise her away from the table and took her off for lunch in the cafeteria. Even here her eyes were opened as she watched how different people coped with their different disabilities. It was all so natural and good-humoured.

Afterwards, Adriana went speeding off in her wheelchair as the rest of us made our way back towards the main hall. When we arrived we saw, to our amazement, that she was already in place at the end of the table-tennis table! "More table-tennis?" we queried, delighted to see such a positive response. "Yes," she replied, so table-tennis it was. We went off to find the equipment. When we returned, we discovered the wheelchair had been pushed to one side and Adriana was **standing** at the end of the table, having obviously realised you can reach so much further when you are upright! There followed another half-hour or so of pure delight. Roy remarked that he had never seen Adriana laugh so much or look so happy.

We were ready for another rest, so suggested we should try snooker, which seemed a gentler game. This was a new game to Adriana. She tended to use the cue as though she was digging for worms which made us a little fearful for the green baize, but we all survived. We did cheat a little as she found it difficult to keep on walking around the table, so we fed the balls back to her. There was great hilarity if we actually got one of them into a pocket.

Next, we decided to watch the swimming. Up again in the lift, then there were some stairs to climb. She made it to the top and then determinedly made her way down all the steep steps to the very front of the viewing balcony so that she had a good view. We tried to persuade her to go in the pool, as there were instructors present, but she steadfastly refused. Swimming was one sport she had really enjoyed before her accident and we thought she might have been happy to enjoy the weightless effect of the water in the company of other amputees. However, she just wanted to sit and watch. We must have been there for at least an hour. In conversation later it became apparent what all the concentration was about. She had been examining every other amputee very closely and comparing their stumps with hers. She was not yet ready to join in fully but was beginning to realise the possibilities.

We were all very quiet and thoughtful in the car on the way home. We ourselves had been amazed and moved by the sights we had seen. We had no means of knowing what effect it had had on Adriana. The facilities we have here for the disabled are often criticised as not being enough but, compared to the lack of facilities in Romania, they were wonderful. We had seen people who, in Romania, would have been destined to spend their lives at home, shunned by society. Instead, because of the treatment, facilities and attitudes here, they were able to live life to the full. Somehow Adriana had to be imbued with that positive attitude before she returned home, if all this work was to be of lasting worth. Could it be done in the time available?

There was no doubt that Adriana had enjoyed her day. She was very happy. Now I had to find the opportunity to break the news to her about the plans for her to go to Thornton College.

20: The real Adriana emerges

The news about Thornton College ruined the rest of Adriana's weekend. I was definitely persona non grata. She was **not** going! She pleaded. She thought of all kinds of reasons why she would be better staying at home and promised she would be very careful not to do anything dangerous. She became angry. She sulked. Lavinia, who had now recovered from her illness and was ready to take her turn on the carer's rota, tried talking to her but got nowhere.

Once more I sat down with Adriana and tried to get through the stone wall she had erected around herself. We looked back at the way all the answers had been provided to previous difficulties, often before we had even asked the questions and again I emphasised how, if God had taken such pains over such details in the life of one person, He must have some very special plan for that person. It fell on stony ground! Adriana was **not** happy and was **not** going to talk about going to school. Perhaps she thought that if she didn't mention it, it wouldn't happen.

We took her back to Oxford with Lavinia on the Sunday afternoon and left them there together, feeling sorry for Lavinia, who was obviously in for a rough time. Grace was to take over on the Wednesday. When I telephoned on the Tuesday evening to see how things were going, Lavinia told me they had talked about the college and eventually Adriana had said, "If this school is where God wants me to go, then I am willing to go"! Not only were we seeing wonderful provision for all the everyday problems which arose but we were being privileged to see amazing changes taking place in the mind and heart of Adriana.

Sheila and I went over to visit Thornton College early that week. It is a convent, situated in its own beautiful grounds, way out in the country. Sister Brenda, the Head Teacher, handed us over to Sister Angela who was in charge of the particular corridor where Adriana would sleep, which was up a steep flight of wooden stairs. There were long corridors between classrooms, common room and dining room. There were also occasional steps along the corridors. It was not going to be easy for Adriana here, but we just knew it was the right place. The sisters struck us as very caring people who were really going out of their way to help us. As Adriana would finish at Oxford just before the college broke up for half-term holiday, she would have a week at home before starting. That was just another detail to be worked out - the important thing was that we had once again found the right place for the right moment. Now all we had to do was convince Adriana of that.

Thursday arrived and it was my turn to stay over in Oxford, ready to bring Adriana home on the Friday at the end of her treatment. I went along to watch her physio session and could hardly believe I was seeing the same girl. She was walking with only one stick, with head erect, back straight, swinging her foot through well and moving along with real grace and ease and with no sign of any lurching or hesitation. As I sat and watched I was filled with a profound sense of gratitude to God for all that He had done. All the work involved and the problems along the way faded into insignificance as I took in what was happening before my eyes. It was a wonderful moment. Adriana was obviously gaining in confidence - these two weeks had worked wonders. One more circuit of the gym and it was time to finish the session. She had worked really hard and, although obviously tired, was extremely pleased with her own progress.

At church we had all marvelled at the fact that so much help had been provided free of charge at the beginning of this project. We had sometimes wondered why we needed all the money that had come in so quickly. Now we were beginning to understand the reason behind it all. Once again we were seeing the wisdom in God's provision. He knew what would be needed - we didn't need to know. Our job was to get on with the job we had been given. These two weeks of private patient treatment had taken a large chunk out of our fund but that was what it was there for and, seeing the new confidence the time in Oxford had given Adriana, it was worth every penny.

The last evening was spent mainly listening to her Cliff Richard tape - by which time I felt *Wired for Sound* myself and had *Mistletoe and Wine* printed indelibly on my memory! Some time previously, knowing what a fan she had become of Cliff Richard, I had written to him explaining her situation and asking if he would send her a word of encouragement. He responded by sending a photograph, with a personal message on it. As I handed the envelope over she looked puzzled. Most of her mail came from her family in Romania, but this was from England. She opened it and looked at me questioningly as she removed the photograph. "Read the message," I said. She found it hard to believe that this was not a hoax but really was from Cliff himself. Once I had convinced her that he had sent it especially for her, the photograph went up in pride of place where all the staff could see it as they came into the room and the Cliff Richard fans among them expressed their envy when they saw it!

With Cliff in the background we spent the rest of the evening doing the English grammar homework which Angela had set Adriana. It kept us both fully occupied. I was so glad I wasn't the one who was having to learn English. I had not realised, until then, just how difficult it can be to think of regular verbs in the English language! We had a good laugh together, so I felt that, by now, I was almost forgiven.

I had taken a brochure from Thornton College to prepare her a little for what was to come. This seemed a good moment to produce it. Adriana took it and looked through it but the atmosphere became distinctly chillier, so I just left it with her. She could look at it in her own time - we were better staying on safer ground with the English grammar.

I left the room to go to the kitchen to make our drinks. When I returned Adriana was sitting on her bed, having removed her legs. At first I didn't take much notice of what she was doing with them, but after a while I suddenly realised she was removing the jeans and putting on the new tracksuit trousers which had been a gift from the head office of a High Street store - just one of the many kindnesses we had received. This was in preparation for the next day. As I watched her I remarked, "You know, there are not many people who can get dressed for tomorrow **before** they go to bed tonight!" She giggled. The legs were now completely accepted as part of her life and she was able to joke about them. "It is my baby," she said, as she cuddled one to her.

The next morning we woke up to snow. Adriana was delighted but I didn't share her enthusiasm as I thought of the journey home to Bletchley and was very relieved when Mary, the physiotherapist, suggested that we should call it a day after the morning session and go home early. The roads were becoming very treacherous and it would not be a good idea to get stuck in a snowdrift with Adriana in the car.

Before we left we had one more visit to make, which was why Adriana had been changing into her tracksuit the previous evening. Andrew, our son, is a journalist on an Oxford paper. He had covered the story of Adriana's visit at the beginning of her stay in the city and his paper wanted to follow it up. I had promised to take her to their office before we left for home so they could take a picture there. I had explained to Adriana much earlier that we had had to make her 'famous' in order to raise the money to help her. She understood and had been very patient with all the people who wanted to take photographs, although she did not enjoy it very much. She agreed to go for this photo-session before we left for home. Having cleared the snow off the car I dug us out of the small drift in the car park and we set off for the *Oxford Mail* office. That particular photograph became the one she prized most - standing in the snow, without sticks or wheelchair in sight, looking for all the world like the normal teenager she is.

Photo-call over, we made our way home. The weather worsened and the roads got progressively more slippery as we neared Buckingham. The last 12 miles from there to Bletchley were pretty awful but we arrived safely. There was no doubt that the two week rehabilitation programme had been a great success. Adriana was walking with much more confidence and was, at last, beginning to chat in English and even initiate conversation occasionally. Real relationships were at last being formed as the real Adriana came into focus.

The following day Adriana transferred yet again to Sheila and Peter's home. We decided that she should make that her base while she was away at Thornton College, so that she would be more settled when she came back at the weekends. She enjoyed having the dog and cats around and it was very easy for her to walk out into the park from their house. We had bought some crampons to attach to her training shoes and it wasn't long before Sheila was telling us that they had been out walking in the snow together and Adriana soon became brave enough to take the dog out for a walk by herself.

There was no doubt in any of our minds that the two weeks' intensive training at Oxford had been a resounding success. The next hurdle we had to face was Thornton College.

21: Many lessons to learn

The fact that Adriana's 17th birthday fell on the day she was to start at Thornton College did not help. What a way to spend your birthday!

A week before she was due to start at the College I had a telephone call from a man from West Wellow in the New Forest area who gave his name as Julian Trinder. A business man, who travels around the country, he had been on his way home from Scotland some days previously and stopped off in Oxford for a meal. As he was alone, he bought a copy of the *Oxford Mail* to while away the time and, on opening it, read Andrew's story about Adriana. Julian felt a particular empathy as he read the story as he himself had, some years previously, been unable to walk for some time due to a leg injury. The picture of Adriana stayed with him and the following weekend, as he passed through Oxford again, he decided to try to visit her. Of course that wasn't possible as we had taken her home for the weekend. Undeterred, he contacted the doctor who gave him my number. Julian wanted to encourage his small church fellowship to pray for Adriana and asked many questions about how she was progressing. Among many other details I mentioned that she had been to the BASA Sports Day and enjoyed table-tennis. I also mentioned that she would be 17 on February 18th.

The following weekend, our daughter Wendy and her husband Mark came to visit us. Adriana was also with us for the evening. Just as the meal was ready to be served, the doorbell rang. There on the doorstep stood a stranger. It was Julian. He had been passing near Bletchley and had decided to pop in with a birthday present for Adriana - a table-tennis bat and balls! Needless to say, an extra place was quickly laid at the table and he was invited to give the present to her personally. As usual, there was very little reaction from Adriana, who found it hard to comprehend why complete strangers should bring her presents and why so many people wanted to meet her. However, I think she was really quite 'tickled' with the gift. It seemed to us that the start of this project had been like throwing a stone into a pool; we had no idea just how far out the ripples would go. We were constantly meeting new people through our work with Adriana and wherever we turned we were making new friends. Julian and his wife, Marion, together with their two teenage children, soon became friends and his small fellowship in West Wellow continued to encourage us with their prayers for Adriana.

We were conscious that a number of our church members might want to mark Adriana's birthday by giving her a small present. Apart from the fact that lots of small presents would only add to the enormous amount of luggage to be taken back to Ploieşti, it seemed that it would be more useful to combine and buy one really worthwhile item. Mihaela, our second interpreter, had let slip one day that Adriana would really like a tape-recorder, so we purchased a radio-cassette recorder which we presented to her in the Sunday morning service. As usual, there was little response but, judging from the number of times Cliff Richard was heard over the following few weeks, it was very much appreciated.

Sunday evening arrived, cold, dark and wet and with it the time to take Adriana to Thornton. Peter, Sheila, Roy and I set off with a very quiet and apprehensive Adriana. We had to use two cars as we also had the wheelchair, piles of bedding, clothes, her mandolin and various other oddments to transport for her stay there.

Sister Angela gave us all a very warm welcome and showed us up the steep wooden staircase to the room which would be Adriana's home for the next few weeks. It was a small rectangular room, like all the rooms on the corridor and contained a bed, chair, table, wardrobe and washbasin. The view from the window was unprepossessing looking out as it did on to the roof of another wing. There was a pin board on the wall and right in the middle of this was a birthday card with a note of welcome from Sister Angela. A lovely touch, we thought, although again there was no obvious response from Adriana who sat quietly while Sheila and I made up the bed and pinned posters and the rest of Adriana's birthday cards on to the board - not forgetting to give pride of place to Cliff Richard's photograph. By the time we had finished, the room looked a bit more homely. There were two small rugs on the polished floor which Adriana immediately pushed under the bed as she could easily have slipped or tripped on them.

By the time all these preparations were completed it was supper-time so we were led downstairs to the large dining room where about six of the girls had gathered. Most of the students would not be returning from their half-term holiday until later in the evening or early on the Monday morning. Sister Angela introduced Adriana to two Spanish girls who took her under their wing as we said farewell. We found it hard to leave as she looked so lost and vulnerable but we had to harden our hearts and just go. We were convinced, even if Adriana was not, that this was the right place for the next stage of her rehabilitation, no matter how hard it might appear to be. I promised to pop in during the week, on my way home from work, to see how she was getting on and with a confidence we were far from feeling, we waved a cheery goodbye and left.

One of our church families had just flown out to Australia for six weeks to visit their relatives and had left their car for our use. Once again the provision came just when it was needed. Without that car I should have been unable to make a promise to visit Adriana mid-week. We enjoyed those few weeks of being a two-car family as it gave me so much more freedom to come and go, popping any letters that came for Adriana in to the College office and visiting her each Wednesday, as well as collecting her on Friday afternoons.

I talked to Sister Angela on my weekly visits. She seemed to feel that Adriana was settling in very well, although she was usually so tired by the end of the school day that she quickly disappeared upstairs to her room and often fell asleep on her bed. The Senior Girls' Common Room was along yet another corridor but she rarely used it, presumably because it was just too much of an effort to get there.

Adriana's assessment of how she was settling in was rather different! "Are you enjoying the school?" elicited a very definite "No!" "What have you done today?" was greeted with a shrug of the shoulders and a pained expression as she replied, "Nothing!" The answer to "Are you getting to know any of the other girls?" was another shrug of the shoulders. Conversation was very much a one-way affair. "Surely you must be doing something - what lessons have you had?" Adriana looked at me and replied vehemently, "English! English! **English!**"

Wisely, the staff at Thornton were soaking her in English lessons. Although she understood enough English to follow conversations, her understanding of the language was not deep or detailed enough to be able to follow the lessons fully. Because of their experience with the Spanish students, the staff realised the best way to help her was to bombard her with English first. It didn't go down very well with Adriana but it made a world of difference as she gained confidence in the use of the language and conversations gradually became easier.

As Adriana's English improved, her mobility also increased along those long school corridors and steep staircase. Not once during her time there did she resort to the wheelchair which we had taken along as 'insurance'.

By this time another BASA Sports Training Day was due. Peter, Sheila, Adriana and I went off once more to spend the day at the Ludwig Guttmann Sports Centre at Stoke Mandeville. We hoped that this time she might be tempted into the pool but she was still not ready for that. After a short time at the table-tennis in one of the small halls we decided to see what was going on in the main hall. Badminton seemed to be the obvious thing to try next so we borrowed a racket. Another amputee, with only one arm, offered to play opposite Adriana, who tried to serve the shuttlecock over the net. She managed once or twice but had great difficulty returning shots as she could not move around the court, particularly as she had handed her walking sticks to Peter while she played. Each time she missed the shuttlecock, it dropped to the floor and one of us had to pick it up and start her off again.

Suddenly a visiting physiotherapist who had been watching, came up behind Adriana.

"Look! You could pick those up yourself," she said.

"No, I can't," was the inevitable reply.

"If you bend this leg like this and lean over like this, you can," she was told.

To our delight, it worked! However, after about ten minutes of this Adriana called for her stick and stamped away to sit on a chair some distance from us. She was obviously not happy. We realised that she probably felt depressed at not being able to achieve more, so left her alone to cool off for a few minutes before going to sit with her.

"What's the matter?" we asked. She looked near to tears as she replied in a low voice, "I can't do it". Just by looking at her face we could understand the mental pain she was going through. Once again we had to gently explain that no one was expecting miracles. Although she may never be able to play badminton, it had not been a negative experience because she had learned, during those few minutes, how to bend down to pick up something from the floor without falling over. That skill would be so much more use to her in the future than being able to play badminton. We sat with her in silence for a few minutes then left her to think things through herself. Before long she joined us again and soon we were back at the table-tennis table, where Adriana took on Sheila and then Peter while I had more than my fair share of exercise by having to run after the balls which missed the table! The real encouragement was to see how Adriana used her new-found technique to collect balls which fell near to her by hooking them with the end of her walking stick then bending down to pick them up once they were within range.

After lunch, we tried pistol shooting. There may not have been many holes in the target cards when we finished but we all enjoyed ourselves. On Adriana's first attempt we were convinced that the only holes in the card were the four made by the drawing pins, so we encouraged her to pretend the target was her youngest brother, Bibi. Poor Bibi was always in trouble for something. As the youngest of nine children, he was not cossetted and spoiled but rather seemed to be the butt of everyone's frustration. When we were in their home it seemed that Bibi had only to appear in the room to be sent out again. We don't know if Adriana visualised him as the

Adriana in the sports hall

target but her second attempt with the pistol was certainly slightly more accurate. Eventually it was time to go home and Adriana very carefully and proudly put away her target cards as souvenirs for her eventual return home - or perhaps to warn Bibi what a good shot she was becoming!

It was now the middle of March 1991 and there was only one more week to go at Thornton. Adriana had coped, although not very willingly at times. On her final day, Sister Angela and some of the girls from Adriana's corridor helped to load all her luggage into the car. I had been waiting to receive a bill from the college but had so far heard nothing. So I sought out Sister Brenda the Head Teacher. As I thanked her for all they had done for Adriana, she asked "Has our Bursar contacted you?" "No," I replied. "That was one of the reasons I wanted to see you, so I can arrange for payment." Sister Brenda waved her hand, dismissively, "No! N! O!" She spelt it for me, so there could be no mistake. My protests that they had not only looked after Adriana and taught her but they had also been feeding her for almost six weeks were brushed aside. Sister Brenda was adamant. "N! O!" she spelt out again, in a tone which brooked no argument. "It has been a pleasure for us to have her and we are glad that we have been able to do a little bit to help Romania." There was no answer to that. It was just another example of the amazing generosity that we were experiencing at every turn.

Sister Angela and the girls escorted us to the car and waved us off as though we were royalty. As I drove home with a very happy Adriana by my side I reflected on the improvement in both mobility and language we had seen during the past few weeks. The time had now come for us to start making preparations to take Adriana home to Romania.

22: Preparations for return

As a result of all the walking that Adriana had been doing, her stumps had shrunk and she was now having to wear three stump socks to keep the legs on. Before we could take her home we would need to go back to Dorset Orthopaedic at Ringwood so that Bob could make her some new, close-fitting sockets.

The week following the BASA Sports Day, Adriana and I travelled down to Ringwood again. This time there were just the two of us. Once again George Buckley had arranged with the hotel and the local Rotary Club for our accommodation and meals. The waiters at the hotel recognised us and were quite amazed to see the difference in Adriana as the last time we had been there she had still been using the wheelchair. As usual we were greeted by members of the Ferndown and Parkstone Rotary Clubs who had always made a point of sending a welcoming committee to see if everything was in order. Bob Watts and his wife Tessa, with their two daughters also paid a social call as did our new friend, Julian. There was no chance of being lonely.

Later that evening we were in our room watching TV and occasionally chatting. The previous week Adriana had fallen in her physio session and had been quite unable to get up from the floor by herself. This is an extremely difficult operation for a double amputee and the episode had obviously shaken her. It was important for her to be confident that if she did fall, once she was home in Romania, she would also be able to get up by herself. We talked this through and decided to ask Bob's advice on how to go about it. Then she could practise when she was on her own in her bedroom, first of all making sure that there was something nearby which she could hold on to by which she could pull herself up. We had a little practise together on the floor there and then but, although it was a most amusing way of spending an evening, Adriana could not get up without making use of nearby furniture. There was unlikely to be a handy bed or chair if she happened to fall on a Romanian pavement - it had to be mastered before she went home.

The next morning, at the hospital, Bob took the necessary plaster casts. I explained the problem Adriana had getting up if she fell down, so Bob lay down on the floor amid all the debris from the plaster and gave us a demonstration of the technique necessary to get up again. He then disappeared with the casts for a long time, leaving us alone in the plaster room. Although normally conversation still did not flow very easily, on this occasion we talked more openly than we had ever done. Inwardly I marvelled at the difference those few weeks at Thornton College had made. Adriana talked quite naturally about her accident and I was able to put together for the first time a much more complete picture of exactly how it had occurred. There was no sense of bitterness or rancour. Although she had suffered from nightmares in the weeks following the accident, these had now completely disappeared.

We talked about her arrival in England and about the first visits to the hospital. Adriana said to me, "You remember when I first wore my legs? I don't know why I got so angry with Bob." She paused and considered for a moment before adding, quite seriously, "But then I was only a young girl of 16." "Yes," I replied, "And now you're a young lady of 17." We both laughed - but there was such a wealth of truth in those words. Bob had already remarked on the difference in her. He had told me very early on that we were going to have to ask Adriana to grow up very quickly and none of us knew if that would be possible. Now it had happened. We could take no credit for it - it was just another amazing change which had quietly been taking place in Adriana's attitude to life.

During this conversation Adriana mentioned that her back had been injured in the accident and she was a bit worried about it. Her mother had also mentioned this while she was here and had asked if it would be possible for Adriana to have an X-ray done. When she was admitted to Oxford I asked her if it was still bothering her, so that it could be mentioned to the doctors. She said it was not a problem now - so we didn't mention it specifically. Now here she was, almost on the point of going home, telling me she was worried about it. Why had she left it until now? She was too afraid to tell the doctors in Oxford, she told me. What could we do at this late stage? Plans were already well advanced for Grace and me to take her back to Romania. The timetable for the final few weeks was filling up rapidly - but we couldn't take her home without having this checked out.

Once we were home, I telephoned Geoff Miller, who agreed to see her at his clinic one evening. He had been such a tremendous source of strength, encouragement and advice but had not yet actually met Adriana. She was extremely nervous about seeing him and was very tense, always turning to me for the answers to the questions he asked - as if I knew where and for how long her back had been hurting. Geoff examined her carefully and arranged an X-ray as a precautionary measure which showed that, although there obviously had been an injury, it had now healed. It would probably continue to cause her some problems, he said, but would not get worse. That was encouraging news and took away another of her fears.

George Buckley invariably came along to the Ringwood Artificial Limb and Appliance Centre when we were there. He was well known to everyone there and his larger-than-life character filled the place with laughter as he teased the nurses and the receptionists alike. Before our final visit to Ringwood for the collection of Adriana's new sockets, George had arranged for the purchase of a new wheelchair for Adriana as a parting gift from the two Rotary clubs who had already shown us so much kindness and generosity. I had not mentioned this to Adriana. It was still usually better to wait to tell her what was happening just before it happened.

It is a long journey to and from Ringwood in a single day so first Anne and then Grace came with us on our last two visits, to share the driving. As we drove down to the hospital on the penultimate visit I informed Adriana that we would be back a little later than usual as we were going to choose a new wheelchair for her. That met with absolutely no response. After the fitting, George led us to the shop from which the wheelchair was to be purchased and they produced several in the right price range for Adriana to try. She just stood and looked at them. "Try them for size," we coaxed. Still she stood there. At last someone said, "Well, sit in one, then!" Adriana stood where she was, dark eyes blazing and said, very decisively, "I don't see why I **need** a wheelchair!"

My eyes met Anne's. We were both thinking the same thing. Was this really the same girl who, only a few short months ago, refused to wear her legs or leave the security of her wheelchair? We wanted to jump for joy but it was not the time nor the place. On the other hand, it did seem rather ungrateful, when someone had offered to buy what was, after all, a rather expensive gift, to turn it down quite so flatly.

Far from being offended by her attitude, George was delighted. "That's my girl!" he said. He was just the right person to cope with it. "Well, if you don't want to sit in it, then I do," he said. "I am tired." Once seated, he carefully explained how delighted we were by her reaction but there could well be times when she would need a wheelchair and it would be better to have one which was her size and comfortable rather than the old one she had at home. He pointed out that, in the hot summer weather, her legs could be very uncomfortable and it would be good to be able to take them off at home and just relax. What if she developed some sores, which can happen sometimes, however careful you try to be. Adriana knew George was speaking from personal experience, so she listened and was eventually persuaded to try the wheelchairs and choose one for herself. It was to be presented the following week on our final visit as George, ever ready to get publicity for the tremendous work he and his friends were doing in Romania, wanted to invite the press for yet another photo-session.

Soon it was time for our final visit to Ringwood. Bob made sure that everything was in absolutely tip-top condition as far as Adriana's legs were concerned. The wheelchair was duly presented by the President of one of the Rotary clubs, wearing his official chain of office. The necessary photographs were taken - but it was George who sat in the wheelchair while Adriana stood behind him with Bob and the President! She obviously had no intention of sitting in a wheelchair again unless it was absolutely essential.

23: Almost ready

There were less than three weeks to go before our departure for Romania and all the travel arrangements had still to be made. There were also lots of other things we had to squeeze into that short time. Everyone suddenly seemed to wake up to the fact that Adriana would soon be going home. In addition, Roy and I had to travel north to Burnley for a family celebration which had been booked long before Adriana arrived.

Colin and Mary Boocock, the people who had first visited Adriana in hospital and who had helped to raise a considerable amount for our fund, came from Derby for the day to visit her. Rod Wallis, who was looking after Lavinia, the Romanian girl who had been so helpful to us, brought her over with her cousin Violetta and took Adriana out on two days. Our church members all wanted to have Adriana in their homes to say their own farewells. The church young people organised a farewell evening in one of the leaders' homes, one of our ladies held a farewell coffee morning - life became even more hectic.

It was important that Adriana should be able to spend some time with the person through whom all this had happened: Pat Boyd, the lady from Seaford, was the link through whom we had first become involved with Adriana's family in 1989. So, eight days before we flew to Romania, Adriana and I boarded the Thameslink train at Bedford, en route to Brighton.

We had to cross the line to board the train, which meant either climbing several flights of steps to cross by the bridge or crossing the track. The latter seemed preferable as Adriana's new sockets were very tight and causing her some discomfort until they were broken in. We booked the tickets and asked if we could have assistance to see Adriana across the track and on to the train. British Rail were very helpful. As we waited for the porter to arrive and escort us over the track, the ticket-collector said to Adriana, nodding in the direction of her walking stick, "What have you done to yourself then? Hurt your ankle?" Adriana looked nonplussed so I replied, "Something like that".

"Never mind, love!" he replied, soothingly. "It'll soon be better." Little did he know! Already Adriana had had several such questions thrown in her direction and she was beginning to realise what a compliment she was being paid. She walked with only a slight limp. There was no way anyone would know by just looking at her that here was a girl with two artificial legs!

It was Adriana's first time on a train since her horrific accident. She said she was not worried as she always enjoyed travelling by train but nevertheless I was a little apprehensive about it. I need not have been. She sat quietly and thoughtfully as the train left the station, then turned to me and asked simply, "Are there many accidents on your railways?" That was all. After that we did puzzles, talked and read. As we passed through London I pointed out the familiar landmarks which could be seen from the train. Eventually we reached Brighton, to find Pat and a welcoming committee of her friends awaiting us. After a meal and the inevitable press photo-session I returned home to make the final arrangements, leaving Adriana with Pat and her husband Ronnie for four days.

Pat travelled back from Seaford on the train with Adriana and then it really was 'all systems go' as Grace and I concentrated on getting mountains of luggage into as small a space as possible. It was only when I tried to lift Adriana's bag and found it quite impossible that we realised just how much everything had been appreciated, although there had been so little expression of thanks at the time. As I emptied the bag to redistribute the load I found that she had kept absolutely everything she had been given, not just the gifts themselves but the wrapping paper, Christmas cards, all the magazines, letters and photographs. Nothing was wasted.

There was already a colossal amount of luggage as we still had some of Olga's surplus baggage to take with us. Now, Adriana was amassing presents by the day, or so it seemed. We pleaded with people not to bring more gifts but there were many kind hearts around and it seemed people couldn't bear to let her go without a gift for herself, her mother or her family: and sometimes all three. We found ourselves packing at least half a dozen teddy bears, talcum powder, magazines, writing paper and chocolates as well as clothes. We also had a wheelchair, bath-board, bath-stool and rubber bath-mats plus all the medical items Adriana would need. Once again RomAF came to the rescue by providing us with documentation so that we could take all the excess baggage free of charge as 'aid'.

While Adriana had been with Pat in Seaford she had played her mandolin in the music group at church and had been given a tape-recording of the service. One evening she wanted me to listen to the tape with her because there was one part where the mandolin could clearly be heard, if you listened carefully. She lay on the floor with her ear to the tape-recorder, urging me to listen. As I couldn't hear it, I got down beside her to listen more closely. Sure enough, there it was - faint but definitely the mandolin. Satisfied that I had heard it, Adriana switched off the tape-recorder and said, "Watch!" As I watched, she got up from the floor, using the technique Bob Watts had shown her on the floor of his plaster room. Unknown to us, she had been practising in her bedroom and had mastered it. She was now completely independent. The depressed, apprehensive girl we had welcomed five months earlier had blossomed into an attractive and confident young lady.

Grace and I were due to stay with Adriana's family in Ploieşti for five days to give us an opportunity to talk to the family and particularly the church about their acceptance of Adriana's disability. We limited ourselves to the absolute minimum amount of personal luggage - nightwear, underwear and a skirt for church on Sunday. Even so, when we arrived at the airport to check-in we found we had 113 kilos of luggage for just three people! The official weight allowance is 20 kilos per person.

On April 19th 1991, just over five months since we met Adriana at Heathrow Airport, we were ready to return to Bucharest. Sheila and Peter came to the airport with us. There were mixed emotions as we waited in the check-in queue. Roy and Stuart were a little anxious about the responsibility Grace and I had for the journey, the Customs and arrangements at the Bucharest end but also very relieved that the 'project' was coming to an end and they might see a little more of us once we returned. Peter and Sheila had come to regard Adriana almost as a daughter and were sad to say goodbye as they did not know when they would see her again. Grace was a little anxious about her two young sons who weren't too keen on their Mum leaving them to go off to Romania. Adriana was excited at the thought of going home. Five months had been a long time to be away from all her family.

It was difficult to work out how I felt: tired, certainly. So much had happened during those five months. The work-load had been quite tremendous and there was still a lot of tidying-up of ends to be done once I came home again. I was mentally checking that no important details had been forgotten and anxious that all the arrangements would go smoothly until that moment when we delivered Adriana back to her family. One thing was pretty obvious - those of us who had been closely involved in the working out of this project had seen God at work in a marvellous, intimate way in one individual's life. We felt very privileged to have been a part of the plan and we had all been changed in some way by the experience.

Rod Wallis turned up at the airport with Lavinia and Violetta who were returning to Bucharest on the same flight, so it was a very lively and noisy party in the check-in queue. The baggage was passed through without any problem. We had booked an ambulance to take Adriana from the

Unaided, Adriana boards the plane as she returns to Romania

terminal to the plane. In this way we could make sure she got on to the plane safely. TAROM, the Romanian airline, do not book seats. Once the flight is called there is a lemming-like dash to be the first on to the plane for the best seats. We could not subject Adriana to that. As soon as the check-in was completed, the ambulance arrived and we were driven off in state to the departure lounge and across the tarmac to the plane itself, where we were boarded first.

Adriana had been carried down the steps of the aircraft when she arrived in November 1990. Now she proudly **walked** up the steps to return home. It was almost a year after her accident. The plane was not fully booked so we were able to push forward the backs of the row in front so that Adriana could sit more comfortably with her legs raised for the three and a half hour journey to Bucharest.

24: Home again

The flight to Bucharest was fairly uneventful, although there was a lot of laughter coming from our area of the aircraft. Adriana sat by the window and could hardly contain her excitement as we passed over the Carpathian mountains and she knew she was almost home.

I had asked for assistance at the Bucharest end of the journey as well as at Heathrow as the flights always seem to land miles away from the terminal building. We had to wait until all the other passengers had disembarked and climbed on to the airport bus before it was our turn.

Suddenly an ambulance screeched to a halt at the bottom of the aircraft steps and a lady doctor, with white coat flapping in the wind and a stethoscope hanging around her neck, rushed breathlessly up the steps and into the plane. She seemed most disconcerted and not a little annoyed to find that the passenger she had come to assist was not only alive and breathing but perfectly capable of managing the steps herself, with a little help. After a sharp word with the cabin crew, she hastened down the steps again and, with a screech of tyres, the ambulance sped off into the distance leaving us still on the plane.

It was pouring with rain by now but at least a young man had been delegated to help Adriana. She managed the steps very well until she came to the final one which was rather steep. As she was deliberating over which was the best way to tackle it her young escort suddenly swept her off her feet and ran with her in his arms to the waiting bus. It all happened so quickly there was no time for her to protest. He bounded up the steps of the bus, deposited her on the front seat and the driver set off for the airport terminal. The passengers watching from the bus had enjoyed that little interlude. So had the young man, who was under the impression he had swept a young English lady off her feet. He was a little disappointed to discover she was a Romanian. Adriana was not too sure how to react but secretly rather enjoyed it. I think it was the first time I had actually seen her blush! The young man made sure we had VIP treatment as we were led to the front of the queue for the first security check, then escorted us as far as the passport control queue before leaving us.

By this time we could see the family waiting way past the baggage carousel and Customs and there were many frantic waves. While we were waiting for all our luggage, we found a man with an empty trolley. At Otopeni Airport that is a bit like finding gold dust, so once we'd found

Adriana arrives in Romania

him we hung on to him. He was very willing to be 'hung on to' by Westerners as it put him in line for a tip - hopefully in dollars. As we collected the luggage together, he chatted to Adriana. She had obviously told him where she had been and what had been happening to her. As the Customs officer asked us to open the first box, the baggage man spoke to him, pointing to Adriana and then to us. We don't know what he said but we and all our luggage were immediately waved through without further scrutiny.

There was only a rope barrier now between us and Adriana's family. Olga was there, plus Faby and Simona. We were almost hauled over the rope as we were smothered with hugs and kisses and had bunches of carnations thrust into our hands. My eyes searched the crowd. Where was Peter? Surely Adriana's father would want to be there for her return? Suddenly I spotted him - standing some little distance away, at the end of the barrier. As I greeted him I was engulfed in a bear-hug which almost lifted me off my feet. Then Peter put me down and turned to watch Adriana **walk** towards him. That was the very special moment he had been waiting for and the reason why he had taken up that particular position. He threw his arms around her and for a few seconds no one else seemed to exist.

Once we were through all the barriers and with the family again the excitement and the noise level grew. Romanians are very inquisitive people and a lot of puzzled glances came our way as we loaded all the luggage into the two waiting cars and set off for Ploieşti, 40 km away.

Our greatest concern had always been how Adriana would ever manage those 39 steps up to the front door of their apartment? Although we had made sure that Adriana had had plenty of practice in walking up and down stairs while she was with us, we were still very conscious of the advice the orthopaedic surgeon had given us even before she arrived in England that it was possible that she would never be able to manage those steps - even if she learned to walk.

When we reached Strada Malu Roşu we were sent on ahead into their apartment block. The men would see to the unloading and carrying of the luggage. We entered the building and, as before, found ourselves in total darkness. Not a glimmer of light on the stone staircase. As we were groping in our handbags for our torches, Grace called out, "Adriana, where are you?" "Here," came the reply, from somewhere up above us." Grace pointed her camera in the direction of the voice and pressed the shutter. The flash revealed Adriana, already part way up the stairs. It seemed as if she had wings, the rate at which she went up. We followed behind marvelling that we had worried unnecessarily. When would we

Adriana climbs the 39 steps

learn that God was in control here? Didn't He know about those 39 steps?

After a lovely meal it was soon time for bed. All rooms in Romanian homes seem to be bed-sitting rooms. Grace and I were to sleep in the living room and Olga hoped we would not mind sharing the bed-settee. We didn't mind as it gave us an opportunity, when everyone else had left the room, to share our thoughts and the many different emotions we were experiencing. It also gave us an opportunity to write up our journals. This was something we were going to have to try to share with the church when we were home again.

We were interested to see what the reaction of the rest of the family would be to Adriana's new legs. Sergius, aged six, the elder of Vasile and Faby's two sons, went to sit on Adriana's knee. Almost immediately he said, "Why is that leg hard?" Everyone laughed. The following morning however, was not so funny. A gloomy Adriana walked into the living room and flopped down on to the settee beside us. "What's the matter?" we asked.

"Oh, nothing . . . just Lily," she replied with a sigh.

Questioned further, it appeared that Adriana and Lily were sharing a room. Adriana, eager for praise, had said "What do you think of my walking?" Instead of the answer she expected, Lily had shrugged her shoulders, waved her hand in a dismissive gesture and said "Oh! So-so." Grace and I could cheerfully have strangled her at that moment. Her attitude was so typical of the Romanian attitude to the disabled. There was no help, no encouragement forthcoming.

Adriana had obviously expected that all the family would be very happy for her and would think she was doing marvellously. We had to talk it through with her again and explain that no one in the family realised what extremely hard work it had been and just how well she had done in such a short space of time. Even Olga, who had been with us for part of the time, did not fully appreciate the amount of effort involved. It was as though they somehow expected that she would return as she was **before** the accident and there was a sense of disappointment that Adriana still needed to use a stick.

25: Back to church

Soon it was Sunday, an important day as Adriana would be going back to her church on her own two feet again. Grace and I wanted an opportunity somehow to speak to the young people and also to the pastor. We had heard, not long after Adriana arrived in England, that some people in the church had told the family, "Of course, Adriana might go to England - but she'll never walk again".

We were dressed and ready for church when Adriana came into the room. She looked very pretty in a high-necked, long-sleeved white blouse and her new navy-blue longer-line skirt and light coloured shoes. She did not like wearing skirts now but we had persuaded her it was better not to cause possible offence on her first week back by wearing trousers in church. She was very, very nervous about her first appearance and confessed she had butterflies. That was an expression she had only recently learned and thought was quite funny.

Grace and Stuart had prepared an 'Open Letter from the Members of Whaddon Way Church to the Brothers and Sisters in Ploieşti Baptist Church'. In it they had listed many of the amazing things we had seen happen after we took on the task of giving Adriana new legs. Many Romanians had the impression that everything in the West is free. It was important for them to realise that this had meant a great deal of work and much kindness and self-sacrifice on the part of many people. We did not want them to feel that they had only to ask and they would receive.

We went to meet the pastor and deacons in the vestry first and handed over the Open Letter to them there. For the two-hour service Adriana, her sister Lily, Grace and I, had to sit on the platform, when we would all have been much happier in the congregation. Once the service was over, many people wanted to greet Adriana and welcome us. We were asked if Grace and I would sing in the evening service and we agreed to do so on condition Adriana sang with us.

Adriana was even more nervous before the evening service. We had asked her to choose what we should sing. If she was to sing with us, it needed to be something she knew. "This one is one of my favourites," she said, pointing to one of the hymns in the copy of *Songs and Hymns of Fellowship* we had taken along with us. As we looked at the words, one of the verses in particular struck us as being most appropriate. It was, in effect, Adriana's testimony to what God had been doing in her life and it read:

Out and about in Ploieşti

You have broken chains that bound me,
You've set this captive free,
I will lift my voice to praise Your name,
For all eternity.

Extract taken from the song I WORSHIP YOU by Carl Tuttle.
Copyright © 1983 Mercy Publishing/Thankyou Music, PO Box 75, Eastbourne, E Sussex, BN23 6NT, UK.
Used by kind permission of Thankyou Music.

When the time came in the service for us to sing, Adriana stood between Grace and me and she coped very well. The pastor welcomed all of us then, to our amazement, read out to the congregation the letter which we had handed over in the morning. It was a long letter but someone had worked very hard that afternoon to translate it into Romanian. After this he turned to Adriana and asked her some questions. She nodded and then looked a little embarrassed, so I whispered, "What is he saying?" She whispered back, "He asked me if I am a Christian." "What did you tell him?" She replied, "I said 'Yes'. Then he asked me if I will join his baptismal class."

That was a question I had not expected - certainly not in front of a congregation of 300, so I whispered back, "What did you say?" "Nothing!" she replied, "It's impossible." (The same old Adriana - 'nothing is possible if I haven't already done it'.) "Why?" I demanded. "My legs," was the not unexpected reply.

This whispered conversation could not continue indefinitely without distracting other people, so I just whispered, "Haven't we learned during the past few months that **nothing** is impossible? We'll talk about this later when we've looked at the baptistry." Then we concentrated on the service once more.

In Baptist churches, baptism means complete immersion in the water, not just a little water sprinkled on the head. A quick look at the baptistry in her church after the service confirmed my worst fears. There were six or seven steps up an iron stepladder on to a small platform about two feet square, then five or six steps straight down into the water. It would certainly not be easy - but a lot depended on how much she wanted to do it! Had she the confidence to believe that it was possible - if she wanted it? Grace and I decided to wait and see if the subject was brought up again.

Vasile and Faby had invited us all for lunch and it was a feast to end all feasts. We realised that it probably meant the family would be on starvation rations for a week or more but it was their way of saying thank you.

After lunch as we were relaxing and playing with Sergius and Emanuel, we realised that Olga and her mother were having a very heated discussion. With Romanians a lively discussion often sounds as if the protagonists are doing battle. This was no exception. Adriana had mentioned about wearing her trousers to church for the evening service. There followed a heated exchange of views between Olga and her mother, accompanied by actions which made it quite obvious, even without an interpreter, what was going on:

Olga pulled her hat down over her eyes, looked pious and then pretended to be involved in some tittle-tattle. What she was obviously saying was "It's no good putting on a 'holy' act in church and then talking behind people's backs". Then, thumping her chest vigorously, she followed up with, "Jesus says that what is in the heart is most important". This is something we had discussed while she was in England, when she had first commented on the fact that the women here did not wear hats in church. Some of the Romanian evangelical churches have a very legalistic attitude to what they consider to be appropriate dress for church. We had explained that we believed what the Bible taught, that man looks on the outward appearance, but God looks on the heart.

Grandmother, with her Bible open in her hands, was poking it vigorously and obviously telling Olga, "But the Bible says . . ." It was great entertainment! Adriana turned to us and rolled her eyes in despair. All she wanted was to wear her trousers to church. We persuaded her that it would be better to wear her skirt until we had had an opportunity to ask the pastor for his ruling on this matter. That seemed to satisfy everyone and harmony was restored.

We had asked for an opportunity to speak to the young people about Adriana informally after the evening service. All who were interested were invited to remain behind. They congregated on the platform where the choir normally sat. It was soon obvious this would not be as informal as we had anticipated as members of the congregation also stayed behind, and eventually we had about 60 people. Claudiu acted as our interpreter. Grace talked about love and acceptance and I spoke about wholeness and normality. We invited the young people to ask questions of us or of Adriana who had bravely opted to stay with us. The idea was to give them the opportunity to ask openly about Adriana's legs, how they were made, how they worked, what she could and could not do. Once their questions were answered, we hoped they would lose any fear of the disability and be more able to accept Adriana back into their midst as she was. They needed to realise that it was going to be possible for her to live a reasonably normal life. There were a few questions, varying from, "how long will the legs last?" and "will they need changing?" to "will she ever be able to drive a car?" and "will she be able to get married?" It was a useful time.

Adriana and family went home while Grace and I went to visit another family from the church whom we had got to know quite well. It was 10.30pm by the time we got back to Olga's apartment. By then, Olga and Adriana wanted to talk!

Adriana was very cross because she said that other people also wanted us to help them. She had said to Olga, "We can't expect them to do that. They have done enough. We must do it ourselves". Her idea was to try, at some point in the future, to start some club or association for the disabled where they could give each other mutual encouragement. That was something positive which we were delighted to hear.

Then she brought up the subject of the baptism again. Was it possible? How could it be done? She could not wear her legs as she must not get them wet. We were pleased that she was thinking through the implications. "So, what's the problem?" we asked. "You have a strong pastor and a strong father. What is to stop you being lifted into the baptistry?" Adriana thought about this, then said, "When you see the pastor tomorrow will you ask him two things for me? Please may I join his class and is it possible for me to wear my jeans to church?"

It was 3am before Grace and I switched off the light and settled down to sleep. It had been quite a day!

26: Time to leave

The following day was spent shopping and visiting, until the evening when Pastor Ioan and Rebeca came to take us to their home for an hour. Once again as I was directed to the front seat I couldn't help recalling the RomAF briefing notes for travellers which advised them never to sit in the front seat of a car next to a Romanian driver if they could possibly avoid it. Faced with that situation, all I could do was close my eyes tightly and pray as he zoomed down the only part of the road where there were no potholes, which just happened to be the middle!

Eventually we arrived safely at their home. As we sat round the table in the hall, talking, we asked Ioan about the possibility of Adriana wearing her jeans to church. A little to our surprise, he was sympathetic to the problem and readily agreed. Then we broached the subject of her baptism, explaining that she would not be able to wear her legs. "That is no problem," he replied, "I can do it in her bath at home." Grace and I looked at each other in horror and simultaneously replied, very forcefully, "No! You can't do that!" They all looked amazed; what was wrong with that idea? We explained that it was very important for Adriana to see herself as normal. She had to be treated as far as possible like everyone else so it was important not only for her, but also for her family and the church that her baptism should be in public. Once they got over the initial shock, they saw the point and we left them to work out the logistics of the exercise.

We were able to go back and report the result of our conversation to Adriana, then it was time to go out yet again for a meal with friends. We persuaded Adriana to go in the wheelchair as it was some distance to walk and she had had a busy day. Faby was so pleased to have Adriana back again that she wanted to help as much as possible, so she elected to do the pushing. All went well until we came to the first kerb when she almost tipped Adriana out of the chair. She then decided the middle of the road, where there were no kerbs, was the safest place. It didn't seem like that to us, with parked cars lining the sides of the roads and the Romanian drivers' propensity to zoom around corners. Faby became so engrossed in the conversation as she walked along that she lost her concentration and steered the chair into a line of parked cars. Adriana was furious, jumped out of the chair with a flash of the anger we had not seen for some time, and stamped off in a temper. It was a frightening experience for her, being helpless to do anything about the danger she saw coming. Faby certainly caught the sharp edge of her tongue and was more or less ignored by Adriana for the rest of the evening. From that moment on, the wheelchair was not used.

After the meal and the socialising, it was time to go back to Vasile and Faby's apartment. There was one more task to be done before Grace and I could return to England and leave Adriana with her family.

For some time we had been wondering how Adriana could finish her education which had been brought so abruptly to a halt when her accident happened. We had talked about this with Olga while she was in England. She pointed out that to reach the High School in Ploieşti required two trolley-bus journeys. That was clearly going to be impossible for Adriana to cope with. In any case she was not yet confident enough in her walking to face the rough and tumble of a large school. A sudden surge of pupils along a corridor or a bag carelessly slung over a shoulder could be enough to send her flying. Trolley-buses also were out of the question. She would need time and space to get on and get off, even if she could manage it at all. Travelling on Romanian public transport is not an easy task even for the able-bodied as it is so overcrowded and there is always a lot of pushing and jostling.

This matter had been given much thought and once again Valerie at RomAF had suggested a possible solution. Since the revolution, several Christian High Schools had been founded in Romania. They were only small and would be a much more gentle introduction back into the educational scene. Pastor Josif Ţon was the founder of the school in Oradea. He had also been the pastor at Ploieşti Baptist Church at the time Adriana was born, so the Dobre family were known to him. Maybe it would be possible for Adriana to start at one of these Christian schools even though there was a great demand for places.

With this in mind, Vasile and Olga were anxious that we should try and get it settled while we were in Ploieşti. We had already tried to telephone Pastor Ţon on one or two occasions without success. On this particular evening Vasile was determined we should try again. This time he was at home and I was able to outline the situation to him. "Which year is she doing?" asked Josif. When we told him she needed to do Year Eleven he was very sorry but said that, as it was a new school, they were only taking Year Ten pupils. Much as he would like to help, it would not be possible.

That was a blow to our hopes. It had seemed that once again, even back in Romania, Adriana's path had already been marked out. Had we made a mistake? Adriana was very quiet and obviously disappointed. So was Vasile, who had been pinning a lot of hope on this school as the solution to a big problem for the family.

As Grace and I talked in bed that night we realised, to our amazement, that in that one day, Adriana had negotiated 18 flights of stairs! We weren't surprised that she was tired - we were exhausted!

The following morning, Grace had the opportunity to talk further with Adriana about school. Eventually they came to the conclusion that, although Adriana had already done much of Year Ten, it would put less of a strain on her to re-do that year's work while she was adjusting to the physical effort of being back at school. That made sense. Adriana said she would write to Pastor Ton and say that she would like to do Year Ten again and I promised to write to him when we returned home. It seemed as though everything was falling into place once more.

Most of the rest of the day Adriana spent quietly at home while Olga took us shopping. Adriana certainly needed the rest but as it was almost time for Grace and I to return to England, Olga was quite determined, despite our protests, that we should take back gifts for almost everyone at Whaddon Way Church.

A final meal with the family in the apartment was followed by a short spontaneous speech of thanks from Adriana, in which she gave us the verse from Psalm 23, verse 1, "The Lord is my Shepherd. I shall not want". Was this really the same person as the helpless, depressed and frightened young girl we had welcomed to England only five months previously? Grace and I were content to return knowing that we had done the job we had set out to do. We realised afresh that God was still in control as far as Adriana's future was concerned. We were just the channels He had been using.

We marvelled at the way everything had come together and the tremendous encouragement it had been to us and our church to see God actively at work in the life of one young person. We had been so conscious of the prayers of our church members as we brought Adriana home. It was a pity they could not all have been there to see how she was settling in. Now, somehow, we had to report all this back to them on our return.

Everyone went to bed and left us to pack what little luggage we now had and prepare for the next day's journey. Even with all the presents that Olga had bought, we still only had one case each to pack, so that took very little time. It took much longer to write up the day's events in our diaries before settling down for the night.

What a good thing that we couldn't see into the future. We slept soundly, unaware that the car booked to take us to the airport in the morning would not arrive. We would eventually manage to reach the airport just in time to see the plane take off without us; spend all day at the airport trying to get a message through to our husbands, who were travelling to Heathrow to meet us; then have to spend two more days with the family before returning to England. However, our missed flight would give us the opportunity to witness to Costel, the young man who had been using his car to ferry us around all week.

27: Meeting with Joni

Roy and I had discovered on our second journey to Ploieşti to see Adriana in 1990 that she had read the book *Joni*, written by a young American woman, Joni Eareckson (now Tada). It is Joni's own story of her diving accident at the age of 17, which left her a quadriplegic, and the struggle she had to come to terms with life in a wheelchair. In particular the book describes her struggle with God and the way He had worked in her life. The book has been translated into a number of languages, including Romanian.

Some weeks after Adriana had arrived in England, we had borrowed the video of the film *Joni* and shown it to Adriana and her mother, with Addy translating. Olga was very moved by the film but, as usual, there was no reaction of any kind from Adriana and there was no way of knowing what impression, if any, it had made.

I wondered if a letter to Joni, similar to the one I had written to Cliff Richard might produce some response which would encourage Adriana to keep on trying when it all seemed too much.

I found two addresses, so wrote to both of them in the hope that one letter would reach Joni. I had heard that she would be visiting Romania in the summer of 1991 as her organisation was hoping to establish some kind of ministry to the disabled, or at least help the Romanian churches to come to terms with and care for the disabled people in their society. I wondered if she would be anywhere near Ploieşti as that seemed an ideal opportunity for Adriana's church and pastor to be given some positive help.

Just after Adriana had left England, the first letter from Joni arrived, so it was forwarded on to her. In fact Joni wrote two letters, both of which Adriana came to treasure. The first was full of understanding of the frustration she knew Adriana must have been feeling and full of encouragement too as she shared her own experience of being in hospital after her accident:

"At night, when visiting hours were over, I fought back tears. That was the only time I could 'be myself' without putting on a fake smile. Deep down I knew that God was somehow part of the answer. But I only had the strength to say to Him 'Show me how to live . . . please.' You might not even be strong enough to pray that kind of prayer right now. It's all you can do to just keep facing another day. But with all the confusion and hurt, try to remember this - God is right with you, caring for you and feeling the hurt right alongside you . . . Life is not easy at your age, especially with a disability. But remember Jesus knows and He understands."

Joni also sent a tape recording of her remarkable testimony. In her second letter she invited Adriana to travel down to the meeting in Bucharest where she would be speaking the following June, and said she hoped to have the opportunity to meet her there.

We realised that life was not going to be easy for Adriana, with her disability, once she was back into normal home life in Romania. We just hoped that she would be able to keep these letters of encouragement and refer to them when the going got tough and her situation looked bleak.

She was thrilled when a member of her church took her, along with Vasile and Faby, to Bucharest to one of Joni's meetings in June 1991, and particularly delighted when, after the meeting, she was able to meet and talk with Joni and her husband. Although they only had a minute or so together, just meeting her was in itself a great encouragement. Joni's husband, Ken, took some photographs of Joni and Adriana together.

Many incidents such as this, small in themselves, have been used to encourage Adriana. Simply seeing the extent of Joni's disability and realising the way God has used her disability to help others was, in itself, an encouragement to keep on going when circumstances were tough and no one seemed to understand.

28: Adriana's baptism

The summer of 1991 passed pretty quickly. After returning from Romania there was a lot of clearing up to be done and still many letters of thanks to be written. Bills needed to be paid and reports written for various publications which had shown an interest. Many of the people who had responded initially to our appeal for funds for Adriana had kept in contact with the situation and needed up-dating from time to time.

We heard from Adriana that Pastor Ţon had agreed that she could start at the High School in Oradea in September 1991. As Oradea is several hundred miles north of Ploieşti, in the north-west corner of Romania near the Hungarian border, accommodation needed to be fixed up so arrangements were being made for her to stay in the home of some members from the Second Baptist Church in Oradea which, with 3,000 members, is the largest Baptist church in Europe. The cost of living was rising ever higher in Romania and Adriana's parents were both receiving pensions. Thanks to the generosity of so many people, even after all medical expenses had been met, we were still in a position to offer sponsorship for Adriana's schooling and accommodation expenses for the first two terms, thus avoiding extra strain on the family finances. Adriana also told us she had started the classes for baptism and would let us know when the date of her baptismal service was fixed.

Adriana spent the summer months acclimatising to her new mobility and gaining confidence. She was now walking confidently with only one stick and, around the home, had no need of sticks at all. When September arrived Olga took Adriana to Oradea to start her studies. The Perţea family with whom she would be staying lived more than half a mile from the school. There was no public transport, even if Adriana could have used it and we were amazed to hear that she was making both journeys on foot. When we enquired about the school, she was very non-committal - but we hadn't expected her to enjoy study after such a long time away.

Eventually, at the end of September, we heard the news that her baptismal service was planned for October 27th. We had promised that, if possible, Whaddon Way Church would be represented at that service, so an open invitation was given to our congregation to see who wanted to go. The response was amazing and by the time all the arrangements were clarified, there were nine of us who could manage it including, to our delight, two of our young people, Suzanne and Anna, plus, of course, Pat Boyd from Seaford, who was not going to miss the opportunity to meet the family on their home ground.

The biggest problems were our diary commitments and the lack of notice of the date of the baptism. However, it was felt by all of us that a special effort had to be made. We had initially decided to 'try to help to raise the money to provide Adriana with artificial legs' and had not looked further ahead than that. We had never dreamed that we would be privileged to see so many other changes in Adriana's life and that we would have had so many bonuses. This occasion was really the icing on the cake as far as we were concerned and we were prepared to do whatever was necessary, so I found myself organising a trip to Romania for 10 people for a **weekend**. The travel agents obviously thought we were slightly mad, as did everyone else we spoke to. If they had seen the amount of luggage we took with us for our weekend trip, it would have confirmed their view.

Stuart took us to Heathrow Airport on a Friday afternoon in October and we were back at Stansted Airport before the shops opened on the following Monday morning. We packed a lot into a very short space of time that weekend, even managing to experience the first October snow in Ploieşti for 40 years.

The flight landed in Bucharest late on the Friday night. We stayed overnight in an hotel and made our way to Ploieşti by train on the Saturday morning, to be met at the station by Adriana and her sister Lily. We had suggested we should book into an hotel in Ploieşti as ten seemed rather a large number to inflict on the family at one time, but they were quite offended at the suggestion. We were all taken to Adriana's home first for a meal before being split into pairs and accommodated by various members of the family and church.

The Perţea family with whom Adriana was living in Oradea made a thirteen-hour journey to Ploieşti in an unheated train, arriving late on the Saturday night. They slept somewhere in Olga's crowded apartment. We never did find out exactly where, but it certainly wasn't in the living room because Roy and I slept there. They made the return journey to Oradea overnight on the Sunday.

Adriana's expressed desire to be able to help other disabled people was given an opportunity of fulfilment while we were there. She and Pat Boyd went to visit a 16-year-old boy who had recently been paralysed in an accident when a rock fell on his back. She did not know him before she went but Pat reported that she was able to bring him encouragement and comfort by her visit.

Before the baptismal service, Adriana confessed to having butterflies again. We suggested she should be still for a moment and reflect over the events of the past year. When she looked back at how many gigantic hurdles she had overcome, this was a very small one by comparison. She reflected for a moment and said simply, "Yes. I know".

Apart from the baptism, Adriana had an extra ordeal to face. She was one of sixteen candidates but, as she had been unable to attend the necessary preparation classes because of the transport problems involved, she had done most of the preparation work at home. Therefore, she had to satisfy the pastor and church of her suitability as a baptismal candidate by submitting to a brief catechism in the service itself - in front of a packed church. The questions began "Who are the three persons of the Trinity?" and continued for several minutes although the rest of the questions were beyond our grasp of the Romanian language. Fortunately, Adriana was facing the choir and, if she faltered, they mouthed the answers to her.

The choir sang several beautiful pieces and, naturally, the English party were expected to do the same. We had come slightly prepared for this eventuality and had managed a quick practice at Olga's home while we were waiting for the meal. We could not possibly match the excellence of the choir's harmonies but we did our best.

For the actual baptism, a high stool was already in place in the baptistry. Adriana was carried up the six or seven iron steps and placed on the stool while giving her response to the normal questions of faith. The pastor then took her in his arms and plunged her beneath the water. The same man who had carried her up the steps was there to receive her back and carry her backwards down the ladder and into the changing room. The logistics of the operation were certainly not easy but the most important thing was that she had had the courage to believe it was possible. It was also important for her whole church to see that it was possible. Adriana was very serene as she gave her responses. It was a moving moment for her family and for all of us who had travelled so far to be there for such a special occasion. There were one or two tears very near to the surface. Once again, we had had proof that, where God is concerned, **nothing** is impossible.

After all the candidates had been baptised and changed into dry clothes they came out on to the choir platform and knelt (all except Adriana, who sat) facing the congregation. Roy was asked to pray for Adriana and the Pastor Ioan and some of his deacons took turns in praying for each one individually. As they prayed, they laid their hands lightly on the head of the person for whom they were praying, as a symbol of the coming of the Holy Spirit into that person's life. At the end of the service there was a lovely touch as some ladies came forward and presented all the candidates with flowers.

Pastor Ioan baptises Adriana

After all the reunion hugs and chats with all our friends in the church, the pastor called for quiet in order to make a little speech in which he thanked us for being there and for the links of friendship which had developed between our two churches. We were very moved as he told us there would always be a very special welcome in their church for any of our members.

We had noticed that Adriana seemed to be in some discomfort when walking and before we left there was opportunity for me to examine her stumps. All the walking she had been doing to and from school had caused them to shrink rapidly and the leg sockets were now too loose. Fortunately, one of the teachers at the school would be giving her a lift to and from school once she returned to Oradea after the baptism, so the problem was not too urgent but we were going to have to set in motion some arrangements for bringing her back to England during her Christmas vacation to have some new sockets fitted.

All too soon it was time to leave. Our train left Ploieşti-West station, the same station on which Adriana's accident had happened eighteen months earlier, at 4am on a bitterly cold and dark Monday morning when the snow still hung heavily on the branches of the trees. Nine of the Ploieşti church members, including Pastor Ioan and Claudiu, waited with us on the unlit platform to see us on to the train and wave goodbye. In spite of the early hour it was a very lively and wideawake party who climbed aboard the train and stood in the dark frost-lined corridor for the two-hour journey back to Bucharest and the flight home.

We were greeted on our arrival at Stansted by Grace, Stuart and family who had not been able to come with us to Romania but had spent all weekend thinking of us. They could not wait to hear all the news of our visit and the baptismal service.

By now it was obvious to all of us that the task we had been given to help Adriana was an ongoing one. The weekend of her baptism may have been the climax to all our efforts of the previous fifteen months but the Lord still had His plans for her future. Our job was to make sure that those plans could be fulfilled by looking after her physical rehabilitation until such time as the necessary treatment could be made available in her own country. Although we had raised far in excess of our original target we knew that money was still going to be needed in the future. As we travelled back to England it was in the certain knowledge that our project was by no means over yet.

29: A setback?

In November 1991, a few weeks after our visit to Ploieşti for her baptism, we had a letter from Adriana. In it she told us that she would not be continuing at the school in Oradea because it was too hard for her. She would be leaving at Christmas. Her letter went on, "It is very hard for me without my family. I am feeling very lonely." My heart sank. What would the future hold for Adriana if she left school now? Would she ever be able to get a job? It was hard enough for able-bodied people to get work now that her country was trying to bring their economic situation up to date. What chance had a disabled girl of finding work if she hadn't even completed her education?

Adriana had obviously realised this but her letter continued, "Maybe I don't have a future but I think that it doesn't matter. God loves me anyway. What do you say? . . . I couldn't imagine it would be so hard. That's why I accept to come to this school."

What could anyone say to that? I rang our committee members and asked them to pray that I would be given wisdom as I telephoned Adriana in Oradea. She was very subdued but agreed to my suggestion to defer making a final decision until she had had time to discuss the situation fully with her family over the Christmas holidays.

Arrangements were going ahead for Adriana to come back to England at the end of December 1991 for a three-week period which was the minimum time in which her new sockets could be made and fitted. It would obviously be best if someone could travel with her, so we invited her sister Simona to come along. We had been concerned about Simona from the moment we had learned about Adriana's accident. She was the one who had found Adriana lying by the track but as far as we knew she had had no counselling or help, instead being left to recover from that traumatic experience on her own. There was little we could do in that situation. Simona did not speak English. However, we somehow had the feeling that if she could just see a little of what had been happening to Adriana in England, by meeting the people and going to the limbfitting centre, it might go a little way towards healing those awful memories.

They arrived at Stansted on December 30th 1991 and we were soon back on the familiar 240-mile round trip to Ringwood. Once again Bob Watts had offered his services free and would only charge for the components needed. He asked Adriana, "Would you like to be taller?" a suggestion which met with an instant "Yes, please!" So she grew two centimetres in as many minutes, much to her delight.

Our church members rallied round again and Adriana and Simona found their free days were quickly filled up. Various people came to see them, they were taken to London for a day and invited for meals in a number of church members' homes. Although Adriana was by now reasonably fluent in English, she found it was not so easy trying to understand, then translate for Simona while still keeping track of the conversation. This meant that for a lot of the time Simona, a quiet but active girl who loves parachuting, skiing and mountain walks, was left in the background. The three weeks of enforced inactivity must have been very frustrating for her, even if they were being spent in another country. We would have loved to show her more of England but there was not the time or opportunity. However, she seemed to appreciate the reason for our invitation and said at the end of her stay that she thought it had helped.

A few days before Adriana and Simona went home to Romania, just after our final visit to Ringwood, Paul and Maxine came to visit them. Paul couldn't get over the change in Adriana. He had not seen her since he brought the result of his sponsored effort 12 months earlier and now he enthused over how well she walked and how good her English was becoming. "What a transformation!" he exclaimed. Everywhere we went, we were hearing the same reaction. At the hospital, Bob had said, "It's hard to believe what you were like when you first came".

Adriana had just laughed at these comments at the time. However, later that evening, just as we finished our meal, she suddenly asked me, "Why did Paul and Bob say I am different now? What is different about me?" What a question! I explained that they meant how much she had grown up in the past year. That wasn't enough for Adriana. "What did people think of me when I first came here?" she asked. How did one answer that, truthfully, in a way she would understand? A little taken aback, I replied, "Why do you want to know that?" It transpired that many other people, on welcoming her, had remarked on the change in her. She couldn't understand what they meant. What **had** we thought of her when she first came to England? **How** had she changed? Now she persisted; she wanted answers!

It seemed as though she had woken up from a very long, deep sleep and was suddenly aware of all that had been going on. How did Bob come to be involved in making her legs when he lived such a long way away? How did George know about her? Why did Ann, the physio, think she would never walk? How did Paul know about her in the first place? What **did** we all think of her when she first arrived?

Although we thought we had explained many things as we went along,

Margaret Cave, Simona , Roy Cave, Adriana, Bob Watts and George Buckley
Photo courtesy of Evening Echo, Bournemouth

they had obviously not registered. Now she was ready and she wanted the truth. We felt that this questioning was good as it was all part of her mental and emotional healing process. The questions and explanations went on for well over an hour.

During the months after Adriana's original return to Romania I had spoken at a number of local churches about all that we had learned through our involvement with her. In response to many suggestions I had started to try to put it down on paper. Adriana knew about this and had been meticulous in making sure that the account of her accident was accurate. Now she wanted to know what else I had written. I told her I had tried to write everything honestly, just as it happened, including all the problems, as it was through the problems that we had really experienced God at work. Eventually, Simona left us to go to bed. As the questions continued I handed Adriana the manuscript, as far as it went, and said, "See for yourself. Everything is there." She took it and disappeared into her room.

The following evening when she and Simona came home from the family they had been visiting they decided to go straight to bed. "An early night?" I asked. "Yes," Adriana replied, "I didn't get to sleep until 3 o'clock this morning." "Why on earth not?" I enquired. "Because I read all of your book" was the reply.

She came back to this subject later. "Will you finish your book with my baptism?" she asked. "Probably," I replied as it had been my intention to finish on that high note. Perhaps that would have been unrealistic, as subsequent events vividly illustrated the difficulties Adriana continued to face once she returned to her own culture.

Adriana told us that she had talked with her family and she had decided to try again at the school in Oradea. She would stay for the full three years until she had finished her education. There was no problem over acceptance of her disability among her fellow pupils. "The people in Oradea have never known me before my accident," she said simply. Looking at her, it was easy to forget she was so disabled. She recalled, laughingly, an occasion when her sister, Lily, had visited her in Oradea. As they walked around the town centre on a cold day, Lily remarked, "My legs are frozen. Are yours?" Adriana stood still and looked at her in amazement. "What did you say?" she asked. It was only then that Lily realised her mistake. Complete acceptance had been achieved, at least in the family.

Shortly after Adriana and Simona returned home in January 1992 we received a letter from Olga, which said:

"At night, when I was reading my Bible, I read from Ephesians 1 v 11-15 and Isaiah 46 vv 10-11. You read them for yourselves and you will see what the Lord said to me about all His blessings."

We turned to the verses mentioned and rejoiced that, at last, Olga too had been able to accept that all things work together for good - even Adriana's accident. The verses read as follows:

Ephesians 1 v 11: . . . In Him we were also chosen, having been predestined according to the plan of Him who works out everything in conformity with the purpose of His will, in order that we . . . might be for the praise of His glory.

Isaiah 46 vv 10-13: . . . I make known the end from the beginning, from ancient times, what is still to come. I say: My purpose will stand and I will do all that I please. From the east I summon a bird of prey; from a far-off land, a man to fulfil my purpose . . .

Olga had had great difficulty in learning to forgive Adriana's friend Raluca for not being able to hold on to Adriana's hand as the train gathered speed on that fateful day when the accident happened - and subsequently denying all knowledge of the incident. Adriana had told us this when Grace and I took her home to Ploieşti and had impressed us both by adding, "I have told my parents they must forgive her. It was no one's fault; it was an accident. I must get on with my new life now with my new legs".

It seemed that life was settling down for all of them at last. They had all accepted what had happened and were looking to the future.

It was just before her 18th birthday in February 1992 when I received another letter from Adriana. It hadn't worked. All the decisions she had made about school and her future had seemed so definite while she was at home with her family but, once back at school, it had not been quite so easy. Now she said, "I went to Oradea and I was happy to go there. I said I wasn't going home until the summer holiday but it wasn't like that. I went to bed and the room was almost empty without my family and I felt lonely again. It's no point staying there and feel so bad. I don't know what will be with me in the future but I am 18 now so I can take decisions by myself.

"I don't want to make you sad but believe me, it's so hard. I thought I could handle this but I couldn't. I'm sorry. My family is sad and you will be sad too when you hear this but you can't do nothing now. When you will receive this letter I will be at home in Ploieşti. I'm sorry for this. Try to understand me, please."

Naturally, all the church was disappointed to hear the news but we had to accept that she had to make her own decisions. At the age of 18 the present often seems so much more important than the future. Who could blame Adriana for giving up if she was so miserable and homesick? She had so many other physical problems to overcome; perhaps she was not emotionally ready to cope with more separation from her family at this stage.

Everyone at our church had been involved with Adriana for so many months and had encouraged her to fight her way through so many difficulties. We had grown to love her and she seemed like part of our church family. Now she was back in her own culture and had to make her own way.

We were all disappointed that, having come so far, she had given up at this stage, but we could not feel that all the work and effort had been wasted. We had been given the task of providing her with legs and giving her the opportunity of taking her normal place in a society where disability is regarded as something to be hidden away. Those 39 steps were the biggest challenge initially - and she conquered them.

She knew it would be hard. There was no easy path and no allowances would be made for her disability in their society. She had amazed all her family and friends by walking again. She had been baptised. She had shown that she could cope with normal life at school. It was the separation from such a large, close family that had been the sticking point.

30: The future?

Adriana was home again but many of her problems were only just beginning. Her family and her own church now had to take the reins and we had to learn to take a back seat and support her by prayer and encouragement from a distance. We knew that, despite all that had happened, this would not be easy as far as we were concerned. We had gone through some anxious and difficult moments while she was here but we had grown to love her. We hoped that the stubbornness and determination which she had shown here would be channelled into constructive activities but there was always the danger that, now she had finished school, she could deteriorate both physically and emotionally. We hoped that we had been able to imbue her with enough confidence to encourage her to enlarge her vision of what was possible. Although she was a bright girl, as a disabled person she would have to prove she was exceptional to stand a chance of getting a job. Did she have enough initiative to push herself? Would her family see the possibilities and help her? Would it make any difference?

In May 1992, three months after Adriana had left the school in Oradea and returned home, I spoke to her by telephone. Communication was so much easier since they'd had a telephone installed in their apartment.

"How are you doing?" I asked.

"Fine," came the reply.

"What are you doing with all this free time at home?" I enquired. There was a pause, then Adriana answered, "Oh, I read; sometimes I go out with my sisters to play table-tennis; sometimes I visit my family." (Gina and Faby, her two married sisters, both live nearby.)

"Anything else?" I queried. "Well, I do my English homework," said Adriana. (Angela Miller, one of our church members, who had helped Adriana with her English while she was with us, was continuing the work by correspondence. It was slow progress but was certainly bearing fruit.)

"And . . . ?" I prompted her. "Well, sometimes I watch television." There was another pause. My heart began to sink a little. Was Adriana really going to be content with such a limited range of activities? Had we set our hopes too high for her?

Then she continued, "Sometimes it's a bit boring".

My spirits soared! I sent up a quick prayer as I replied, "Maybe that's because you don't have the kind of structured day you have been used to at school. Is there no possibility of you going back to school in Ploieşti? It would fill up your days for you and you would meet more people."

Why had I said that when I already knew the answer to that question? Sure enough, Adriana replied, "That's not possible because I would need to catch two trolley-buses and I can't do that." An impulsive thought came to me as if in immediate answer to my prayer and I asked her, "How much would it cost to go by taxi?"

"I don't know, but it would be very expensive."

"Be careful here, Margaret" I thought. "You are not the Big Boss any longer. Remember she's 18 now and makes her own decisions." Phrasing it as tactfully as possible I replied, "I know it would be too expensive for you but, as we are no longer having to pay school fees for you in Oradea, we could use that money to pay for a taxi for you to go to school - if you would like to. If you think that is a good idea, talk to your family about it and see how they feel. Then let me know if you think it would work."

We talked for a minute or so about the rest of the family and I rang off. The next day, in our morning service, the congregation was asked, "Has anyone got anything they want to thank God for?" "Yes," I replied, "Let's thank Him that Adriana is getting bored at home. Another answer to our prayers." Everyone laughed but they understood the underlying message.

A week or so later a letter arrived from Adriana. The family had talked the matter over and would accept our offer to pay taxi fares. Her letter said, "I can go to a high school in Ploieşti but I have to pass an exam, so if I will take the exam I can go to school. It will be very hard but I will try." That was more like the Adriana we had taken home to Ploieşti.

We sent out the money towards the first term's taxi fares - with their rate of exchange it was incredibly cheap - and on 15th September 1992 Adriana re-started school. On 22nd September she wrote, "I go to school in the afternoon from 1.30 - 7.15pm. I learn in a classroom on the second floor. Magda (her younger sister) is going to the same school in the mornings from 7.30am - 1.30pm. I was lucky I didn't have to start school so early."

In October, another letter arrived. "The school is going on just fine. Certainly here in Ploieşti it's much more better than Oradea."

The first term passed. In January 1993 we received an encouraging letter from Vasile, which read "Adriana is fine and she is doing OK at school. It seems that at English she is good. For Adriana sometimes are hard moments, but these moments must be overcome."

In March 1993 a short letter from Olga and Peter acknowledged receipt of the money for the taxi fares up to the end of the school year and said they would also use the taxi to take Adriana to church each week - a very sensible idea we thought, particularly if they could cram a few more of their large family into the same vehicle! However the part of the letter which gave us the greatest encouragement said:

"Adriana's school is going on just fine. She realised how important is this school and we realised it too."

Another prayer answered. Adriana was not just going to school to fill in her days but had actually realised the importance, in her situation, of continuing her education.

In June 1993, Adriana completed a full academic year. After missing two years as a result of her accident, to our delight she decided to return to school in September 1993 for a final year, even mentioning the possibility of going on to university later.

Since Adriana first returned to Ploieşti, many people have asked us the same kind of questions that we have been asking ourselves: What will happen to her in the future? Will she ever be able to complete her education? Will she ever find employment? We have no way of knowing the answers to most of their questions but when we returned Adriana to her home, family and church in April 1991, part of the 'Open Letter to Ploieşti Baptist Church' which Grace and Stuart compiled summed up our feelings:

"For us it has been a privilege to be involved in what God has done . . . Our faith has been strengthened and our vision widened. Our church has done what we can and we lovingly bring Adriana home to your care.

We, at Whaddon Way Church, have had the privilege of being used in the initial rehabilitation part of God's plan for Adriana. You, our brothers and sisters in Ploieşti Baptist Church, now have the challenge and responsibility passed back to you. We commit her to your love and care. We look forward to hearing how the Lord continues to move among you as you meet the many challenges He has set before you now."

The letter we received in reply was encouraging:

"We here at Ploieşti Baptist Church accept the challenge that you have passed on to us. We promise before all mankind to receive Adriana openly, to encourage her to live that normal life, which is full of blessings from God. We vow to one and all to love, uplift and continue the work of God in her life. Each one of us can say, 'God is not finished with me yet: please be patient with me'."

God has not finished with Adriana yet - of that we are certain!

Postscript

It would have been hard to believe when Adriana first came to England in November 1990, that in October 1993 she would be returning, not just for a necessary change of sockets for her limbs, but also acting as the interpreter for another member of her church.

Mihai Teodorescu, a 25-year-old Romanian welder lost a hand in November 1992. How? In a train accident! Since his father's death in 1988, Mihai had been the sole support for his mother and sister. He desperately needed an artificial hand.

When Ploieşti Baptist Church appealed to us for help, we looked at the amount still available in the 'Adriana' fund. There was exactly £4,000 - the amount we had originally set out to raise for Adriana when we made that tentative decision to 'do all we can' in May 1990! Some people would call that coincidence - we believe it was God's confirmation to go ahead in faith.

It seems that God has not finished with Whaddon Way Church either . . . but that's another story!

ADRIANA

You came to this land
Under a shadow, cold of heart,
With frozen memory;
You, a silent stranger
With angry words, withdrawn,
Gripped by a lack of freedom.

Your sad eyes were so sombre.
Such clouds of the mind
Tumbling, rolling, consuming,
Lingering, swirling shadows:
How could you smile
With a young girl's grief?

But so many hearts of England,
Like a waterfall touched by sunlight
That could be heard across the land,
Covered you in love and care,
And to God came so much prayer
To take away your hurt.

So, precious time gave back your smile;
Now, freely given and quickly caught:
Rearranged the paths, of new freedom found,
In shining threads of love and prayer:
Others will need you now,
Reborn soul and fearless heart.

Departing from this English soil
A woman you became:
No princess of royal blood
But a princess of the heart:
England's wish, so much hope for you:
Romania, Romania, takes you back with love.

Dedicated to Adriana Dobre, 19th October 1991
by Ronald M Boyd, Seaford, England